LEADERSHIP
AND
CHURCH
ORGANIZATION

WISLY PERICLES

WESTBOW
PRESS®
A DIVISION OF THOMAS NELSON
& ZONDERVAN

Copyright © 2020 Wisly Pericles.

All rights reserved. No part of this book may be used or reproduced by any means, graphic, electronic, or mechanical, including photocopying, recording, taping or by any information storage retrieval system without the written permission of the author except in the case of brief quotations embodied in critical articles and reviews.

WestBow Press books may be ordered through booksellers or by contacting:

WestBow Press
A Division of Thomas Nelson & Zondervan
1663 Liberty Drive
Bloomington, IN 47403
www.westbowpress.com
844-714-3454

Because of the dynamic nature of the Internet, any web addresses or links contained in this book may have changed since publication and may no longer be valid. The views expressed in this work are solely those of the author and do not necessarily reflect the views of the publisher, and the publisher hereby disclaims any responsibility for them.

Any people depicted in stock imagery provided by Getty Images are models, and such images are being used for illustrative purposes only. Certain stock imagery © Getty Images.

Scripture taken from the King James Version of the Bible.

ISBN: 978-1-6642-0930-5 (sc)
ISBN: 978-1-6642-0931-2 (e)

Print information available on the last page.

WestBow Press rev. date: 11/03/2020

Contents

I

Introduction

L EADERSHIP IS AN ESSENTIAL TOOL THAT GOD HAS GIVEN TO
human beings to maintain His creatures. He has created us
with the ability to administer the cosmos included all things
that He has made. His seven days of creative activities are an
administration sample and clearly explain His leadership; His
organizational leadership allows Him to set up a schedule for
each day to make perfect His work. "By the seventh day God had
finished the work he had been doing; so on the seventh day, he
rested from all his work" (Genesis 2:2).

In the book of Genesis, God demonstrated an excellent
methodology, which is the administration of time. He has, as a
Supreme Scientist, determined what to do in each day. He has
questioned each thing that He has made; He has tested it. He
has analyzed before concluded. For example, "…And God said,
'let the land produce living creatures according to their kinds:
livestock, creatures that move along the ground, and wild animals,
each according to its kind.' And it was so. According to their
kinds, God made wild animals and all creatures that move along
the ground. And God saw that it was good" (1:24-25). God is so
wonderful!

As an organizational leader, He has created everything before

He has created Human beings. Then, He has given human being a sample of organization, and He chose him as the administrator of His creatures. "Let us make man in our image, in our likeness, and let them rule over the fish of the sea and the birds of the air, over the livestock, over all the creatures that move along the ground" (1:26). "Now the Lord God had formed out of the ground all the beasts of the field and all the birds of the air. He brought them to the man (the trainee organizational leader) to see what he would name them; and whatever the man called each living creature, that was its name. So the man gave names to all the livestock, the birds of the air and all the beasts of the field" (Genesis 2:19-20). The organizational leadership' trainer gave the trainee all information required to be an excellent corporate leader.

Consequently, each human being is a leader. Still, if one thoroughly understands the leadership that God has demonstrated in creating the universe, he/she would be a great organizational leader. This book will teach you that God, Elohim, is not an authoritarian leader because one God in three persons, triune, has created the cosmos. He is a transformational leader because He has transformed human life. He likes to share power as a democrat. He is a visionary leader because He is omniscient, He knows how tomorrow will be and what human being or a community needs tomorrow to function normally. Then we must follow God's path if we want to be a great and successful leader.

II

Leadership: Definition

L EADERSHIP IS THE EXERCISE OF AUTHORITY, EXPLAINED
Shafritz, whether formal or informal, in directing and
coordinating the work of others. The best leaders are those
who can simultaneously exercise both kinds of leadership: the
formal, based on the authority of rank or office, and the informal,
based on the willingness of others to give service to a person
whose special qualities of authority they admire. It has long been
known that leaders who must rely only on formal authority are at
a disadvantage when compared with those who can also mobilize
the informal strength of an organization or nation (Shafritz et
al, p. 385). It is sine qua non to know what you are doing, and
it is difficult to do something that you ignore what it is or be
in a position that you ignore all requirements of that position.
To understand better the meaning of leadership, Crosby (2005)
has enumerated the following concepts: understanding the
social, political, economic, and technological givens as well as
potentialities (p.34).

"Leadership is the performing art in which self is the vehicle,
says Boldman. In some ways it's like acting. In knowing who I
am, knowing something about how people see me, knowing what
I care about, what my goals are, or what's important to me, I can

understand who I am as a leader" (BizEd, November/December, 2003). Leadership is the ability to control the surrounding environment, whatever it is, and do not let it influence you, but you shape it as a leader.

Leaders (Crosby & Bryson, 2005) ensure that the organization develops flexible, transparent, just, and compassionate governance, administrative, and employee – development systems that develop and sustain the organization's core competencies (Light 1998; Collins and Porras, 1997). The organizational systems should also allow conflict to surface, so that the organizational is able to learn from varying perspectives, support organizational members' efforts to carry out the mission, and respond to stakeholder needs (p.87). Leaders from different organizations should elaborate on their organization system and all barriers they have faced and how they have overcome them. Crosby & Bryson (2005) assert that Policy entrepreneurs need visionary leadership skills as they organize forums (face – to – face and virtual) in which key stakeholders (many of whom represent a group of stakeholders) can develop at least a preliminary shared understanding of the problem and why doing something about it is important, and possibly urgent (p.170). Then 'Redefining public service' needs visionary leaders; without them, no one might redefine public service.

An organization's purpose and connected core values (Crosby & Bryson, 2005) serve as the collective raison d'être for everyone there, as a way of framing reality and as guiding compass for choosing direction. Continual, explicit attention to purpose and core values is especially important in any large, decentralized organization (p. 81). All organization members are important; their collaboration to each other could enhance the production of the organization. Even though the stakeholders and all leaders may have different views, they should compromise for the organization's benefit. Each human being has his/her own view on everything; leaders or collaborators in an institution should never surprise to face different view vis-à-vis a subject that should seem clear and understandable. We have always heard from others: it is a dawn question, it is a dawn answer, it is a dawn viewpoint; that is right! Because we are human beings, we see everything differently.

The phrase organized anarchy (Crosby & Bryson, 2005) has been used to describe the disorder, confusion, ambiguity, and randomness that accompany much decision making in large, "loosely coupled" organizations (Cohen, March, and Olsen, 1972). The term applies, perhaps with even more force, to the shared - power, interorganizational, interinstitutional policy environments where no one is in complete charge, and many are partly in charge (p, 161). Without compromising, the organization will go nowhere. All successful organizations do not mean they do not face any ambiguity between their members, but all members agree to collaborate with the organization's progress.

In 1999 (Shafritz et al.,2009), the National Academy of Public Administration (NAPA) established a priority issues task force to identify the key issues in public administration that would face the nation in the first years of the twenty-first century. What the task force found was that governance throughout the United States and around the world was "undergoing a fundamental transformation" that had huge implications for public administrators (p.160). A leader or a group of leaders' role is to evaluate what they did to determine if the job was not well done and what they should do for the enhancement of the organization. NAPA identifies the keys issues as a macro public administration association. Still, a church leader should always identify and observe what is not going well and fix it quickly. A chief administrator, pastor should meet all his/her collaborators to identify the problem and find a solution as soon as possible. A decisive leader does not see a question and lets the administration function to pretend the problem will be solving by itself or waiting for an appropriate time to fix it. This behavior is harmful. It is so funny when a church leader says: let it that way, God will fix it. It looks like those leaders do not read

Genesis 1:26-27: Then God said, Let us make man in our image, in our likeness, and let them rule over the fish of the sea and the birds of the air, over the livestock, over all the earth, and overall the creatures that move along the ground. God created man in His image; He created him; male and female he created them. Then we are created with God's image, we have the intelligence and knowledge of God even our knowledge is limited, but God gives us the ability to think, lead, and control everything. God would intervene only in a problem that surpasses our capacity to resolve, but God will not do anything if the problem does not exceed our ability to be solved.

A process framework (Stillman II, 2010) for collaboration suggests that collaboration occurs over time as organizations interact formally and informally through repetitive sequences of negotiation, development of commitments (p.288). A church organization is under the control of a team leader; all leaders would know each other every day by interaction. The subaltern should respect the Pastor and their leaders and do their best to understand their character allowing the collaboration to be more comfortable and successful. The primary key to the success of an organization is commitment. Suppose all members of the organization committed to developing their organization. In that case, they should be positive and have the determination to achieve their goals, whatever the circumstances or inconveniences they might find.

Few concepts (Stillman II, 2010) are debated in administration more frequently than decision making – how decisions are made; whom they are made by; why they are decided on in the first place; and what impact they have once the choice is made (p.212). Consequently, many factors might be developed in decision-making such as policy development, implementation, and evaluation. Implementation, or operationalization, (Crosby & Bryson, 2005) of change typically is a complex and messy process involving many actors and organizations with a host of complementary, competing, and often contradictory goals and interests (Goggin, Bowman,Lester, and O'Toole, 1990; Peters and Pierre, 1998,2003). Clearly, policy implementation must be planned, facilitated, monitored, and evaluated (p.312). A policy cannot implement without those steps mentioned above. According to Crosby & Bryson (2005), in the implementation and evaluation phase, policy entrepreneurs must prepare for a shift in the advocacy coalition's composition that supported the adopted policy change in earlier phases. Some coalition members may be ready to move on to another pressing social need or problem, or their job may change (p.314). Policy implementation remains one of the great concepts of administration. 'Redefining public service through civic engagement' cannot be efficient without thinking about reviewing the concept of policy implementation. Many events in the 21st century encourage public administrators to think about new policies and implement them, such as the 911 attacks and Katrina Disaster. Both have allowed local and federal governments to make decisions to avoid any eventual attacks and disasters like the previous one.

According to Crosby & Bryson (2005), in the implementation and evaluation phase, policy entrepreneurs must prepare for a shift in the composition of the advocacy coalition that supported the adopted policy change in earlier phases. A policy cannot execute without those steps that I mentioned above. The church administration is like any other administration, private or public; do not think it should not organize very well. If we refer to the history book of the primitive church, Acts, we will see how it functioned very well. Some members of the coalition, argued Crosby & Bryson, may be ready to move on to another pressing social need or problem, or their job may change (p.314). Policy implementation remains one of the great concepts of administration. 'Redefining public service through civic engagement' cannot be efficient without thinking about reviewing the idea of policy implementation. Many events in the

21st century encourage public administrators to think about new policies and implement them, such as the 911 attacks and Katrina Disaster. Both have allowed local and federal governments to make decisions to avoid any eventual attacks and disasters like the previous one. It is the same scenario for a church administration. The pastor should think about adopting new policies according to the need of the church. The group leaders should do the same, but they cannot take any decision without informing the pastor and the committee. It depends on the kind of changes because the group leaders are the pastor's collaborators; they should not and cannot implement any policy or decision that could negatively affect the church administration. As Jethro said to Moses: "… have them bring every difficult case to you; the simple cases they can decide themselves" (Exodus 18: 22).

III

Systems Theory

Accdording to Shafritz, systems theory views an organization as a complex set of dynamically intertwined and interconnected elements, including its inputs, processes, outputs, feedback loops, and the environment in which it operates and continuously interacts (p. 255). The church, as an organization, has subdivided into many mini-organizations. The church gets a macro administration. The mini-organizations have a micro administration; all administrations in the church organization interconnect to develop a well-organized organization (church or mission). A CEO (chief executive officer) does not have to tell anyone that his/her organization is in good shape; the production or performance of that organization is her Porte-parole. The creation or execution is the cue to indicate the health of the organization. It is the same observation for a church; when you enter a sanctuary, you know if it is in good or bad health spiritually and administratively. The interconnection of all activities and sections is vital for keeping healthy a church or mission or any other organization. You do not have to be a musician to determine if the orchestra performs perfectly or not if the choir sings well or not.

IV

Trait Theories

PERSONALITY CHARACTERISTICS REMAIN A CRITICAL ASPECT to determine the level of the potentiality of a leader. Shafritz et al. (2009) argue that the trait approach to leadership assumes that leaders possess traits—personality characteristics—that make them fundamentally different from followers. Advocates of trait theory believe that some people have unique leadership characteristics and qualities that enable them to assume responsibilities; not everyone can execute. Therefore they are born leaders (p.389). Then leadership is a gift received by God; it is innate. However, every person has his/her character; then, someone's character would determine how he/she can assume some responsibilities. For example, Peter was different than other disciples due to his nature. Some social scientists focus on characterology (which is an area of personality psychology) to determine the character or trait or behavior of human beings. However, others do not consider characterology as a science.

According to Princeton University, Personality psychology is a branch of psychology that studies personality and individual differences. Its areas of focus include:

- Constructing a coherent picture of a person and his or her major psychological processes.
- Investigating individual differences, that is, how people can differ from one another.
- Investigating human nature, that is, how all people's behaviour is similar (http://www.princeton.edu/~achaney/tmve/wiki100k/docs/Personality_psychology.html)

A. TYPES OF LEADERSHIP

The trait of a leader could determine, according to some scientists, what kind of leader that person is; if he/she is a strong or weak leader. I do not believe in characterology or personality psychology because trait or the portrait of your face cannot influence your performance if you receive a calling from God. It does not matter who you are; God can transform you to make you how He wants you to accomplish a special mission. However, most of the time, God can choose someone whatever his/her trait allows him/her to achieve what people do not expect. A human being cannot limit the power of God. Don't be frustrated about your calling; God does not choose anyone for his/her capacity or ability. His twelve disciples remain a great example; most of them were fisher; they did not know laws compared to Pharisees, Sadducees, and scribes, but God taught them and made them superior to those guys. It does not mean that God does not believe in knowledge, but He wants human beings to recognize that He is the knowledge and possesses the sum of experience and can transfer His knowledge to whom He wants to.

There are different leadership types, such as authoritarianism, transformational leadership, Moses leadership, Jethro leadership, Charismatic leadership, Moral leadership, organizational leadership, Visionary leadership, democratic leadership, team leadership, etc.

1. Authoritarianism

Authoritarian leaders determined all policies, set all work assignments, were personal in their criticisms, and were product (or task) oriented. Democratic leaders shared decision-making powers with subordinates, left decisions about assignments up to the group, and participated in group activities but tried not to monopolize. They exhibited high levels of consideration for others. Laissez-faire leaders allowed freedom for individual and group decision making, provided information (or supplies) only when requested, and did not participate in the group except when called upon. They functioned more as facilitators (Shafritz et al, p. 391).

Authoritarian leaders act as dictators; they decide what should be done without thinking about their collaborators' advice. They aim only to achieve their goals. Most of the time, their collaborators are considered dummies or robots; they do exactly what their leaders want to. They do not have self-esteem; they do not think about their personality. They work only for their reward. What is good for the boss is right for them. If their boss fails, they fail too. Ahab's false prophets remain a great example of an authoritarianism regime; their king, Ahab, wants to invade Ramoth without consulting Elohim. He has taken that decision on his own without consulting the Lord and his people. Then the people included the prophets (false) agree with him without any question. He asks Jehoshaphat to help him fighting against Ramoth; however, Jehoshaphat would like to support him, but he asks him to inquire for the word of the Lord. Then the king of Israel gathered the prophets together, about four hundred men, and said to them, Shall I go against Ramoth Gilead to fight, or shall I refrain? So they said, Go up, for the Lord will deliver it into the hand of the king. (I Kings 22:6). Jehoshaphat, the servant of God, does not think that their answer comes from God; he said: Is there not still a prophet of the Lord here, that we may inquire of

Him? So the king of Israel said to Jehoshaphat, There is one man, Micaiah the son of Imlah, by whom we may inquire of the Lord; but I hate him, because he does not prophesy good concerning me, but evil. And Jehoshaphat said, Let not the king say such things! Then the king of Israel called an officer and said, Bring Micaiah the son of Imlah quickly! The king of Israel and Jehoshaphat the king of Judah, having put on their robes, sat each on his throne, at a threshing floor at the entrance of the gate of Samaria; and all the prophets prophesied before them. Now Zedekiah the son of Chenaanah had made horns of iron for himself; and he said, Thus says the Lord: With these you shall gore the Syrians until they are destroyed. And all the prophets prophesied so, saying, Go up to Ramoth Gilead and prosper, for the Lord will deliver it into the king's hand (I kings 22: 7-12).

The statement above demonstrates two elements of an authoritarian regime: blindness fanatic and dishonest. The false prophets know that they do not receive any words from God, but they want to force the prophet to repeat their words. The king of Israel, Ahab, is not honest; he does not have morals. He declares that he hates the prophet because he does not say any good things for him, but he ignores that the prophet speaks God's words, not his own words. It is the characteristic of all authoritarian leaders; they do not accept the freedom of speech. They like only dummies.

Then the messenger who had gone to call Micaiah spoke to him, saying, "Now listen, the words of the prophets with one accord encourage the king. Please, let your word be like the word of one of them, and speak encouragement." And Micaiah said, "As the Lord lives, whatever the Lord says to me, that I will speak." Then he came to the king; and the king said to him, " Micaiah, shall we go to war against Ramoth Gilead, or shall we refrain? And he answered him, " Go and prosper, for the Lord will deliver it into the hand of the king!" So the king said to him, " How many times shall I make you swear that you tell me nothing but the truth in the name of the Lord?" Then he said, "I saw all Israel scattered on the mountains, as sheep that have no shepherd, and the Lord said, "These have no master. Let each return to his house in peace.'" And the king of Israel said to Jehoshaphat, "Did I not tell you he would not prophesy good concerning me, but evil?" "… Therefore look! The Lord has put a lying spirit in the mouth of all these prophets of yours, and the Lord has declared disaster against you." Now Zedekiah the son of Chenaanah went near and struck Micaiah on the cheek, and said, "Which way did the spirit from the Lord go from me to speak to you?" And Micaiah said, "Indeed, you shall see on that day when you go into an inner chamber to hide!" So the king of Israel said, "Take Micaiah, and return him to Amon the governor of the city and to Joash the king's son; "and say, 'Thus says the king: "Put this fellow in prison, and feed him with bread of affliction and water of affliction, until I come in peace.'" But Micaiah said, "If you ever return in peace, the Lord has not spoken by me." And he said, "Take heed, all you people" (I Kings 22: 13-28)!

An authoritarian leader cannot be a democrat; he is always a dictator. Chenaanah struck Micaiah on the cheek because he told the truth to the king, and the king also put the prophet of God in prison. I focus on Ahab story to help my readers understanding better the characteristics of an authoritarian leader. There are many authoritarians' leaders in the world history such as Adolf Hitler, Mussolini, Idi Amin Dada, Francois Duvalier, and so on.

Hitler, after legally gaining power in Germany, he quickly began solidifying his position putting those that disagreed with him into concentration camps. He created massive amounts of propaganda that strengthened German pride by blaming all their problems on Communists and Jews. The concept of pan-Germanism inspired Hitler to combine German peoples in various countries in Europe as well as look east for lebensraum. Since the world was extremely sensitive about the possibility of starting another war, Hitler was able to annex Austria in 1938 without a single battle. But when he had his forces enter Poland in August 1939, the world could no longer stand aside and just watch—World War II began. From the Nuremberg Laws in 1935 to Kristallnacht in 1938, Hitler slowly removed Jews from German society. However, with the cover of World War II, the Nazis created an elaborate and intensive system to work Jews as slaves and kill them. Hitler is considered one of the most evil people in history because of the Holocaust (www.history1900s.about.com/cs/hitleradolf/p/hitler.htm). Hitler's trait expresses that he is an authoritarian leader or a dictator; he tried to kill all his opponents, which is normal characteristic of an authoritarian leader.

Idi Amin Dada Oumee was the president of Uganda from 1971 to 1979. They considered him as one of the cruelest despots in world history. His regime killed more than 300,000 people.

Groups with democratic leaders were the most satisfied and productive. The authoritarian-led groups showed the most aggressive behavior and were the least satisfied, but they were highly productive (possibly because of fear of the leader). The groups with laissez-faire leaders showed low satisfaction and low production, and they were behaviorally aggressive toward group members and other groups. Thousands of subsequent studies have essentially presented the same findings—democracy, meaning participative management, works (Shafritz et al., p. 391).

Managers with authoritarian personalities and styles value order, precision, consistency, obedience, rules, law, and organization. To them, the power that flows from structure is supreme. Relationships are hierarchical, based on dominance and dependence. Authoritarianism, control through structure, is rigidly unbending. Yet authoritarians, while often initially successful, cannot survive over the long term. Whether large scale (such as Hitler or Stalin) or pint sized (such as an oppressive supervisor), authoritarians will ultimately fail because "democracy is inevitable." It is inevitable not just because it is good but because it is more effective—especially in the modern world, with its high-tech workforce. In the meanwhile, however, authoritarians cause considerable psychic damage in individuals and generate lost productivity in the internal organizational polity while often sustaining **authoritarianism** in the outside polity (Shafritz et al., p. 391).

authoritarianism Rule by an individual whose claim to sole power is supported by subordinates who sustain control of the system by carrying out the ruler's orders and by a public that is unwilling or unable to rebel against that control. The ruler's personality may be a significant element in maintaining the necessary balance of loyalty and fear. Authoritarianism differs from totalitarianism only in that the latter may have a specific ideology that rationalizes it, although it may require a leader who embodies that ideology to sustain public support. An authoritarian state may be further distinguished from a totalitarian one by the fact that under some circumstances an authoritarian state could allow limited freedom of expression and political opposition, as long as the regime does not feel threatened (Shafritz et al, p. 391).

2. Transformational leadership

A transformational leader is one with the ability to change an embedded organizational culture by creating a new vision for the organization and marshalling the appropriate support to make that vision the new reality. The best-known transformational leader is General George S. Patton Jr., who during World War II took charge of a defeated and demoralized American Army in North Africa and transformed it into a winning team. The task was different but no less difficult for Lee Iacocca when he took charge of a Chrysler Corporation on the verge of bankruptcy and disintegration in the late 1970s and brought it back into profit. Similar challenges faced the leadership of AT&T in 1984 when it went from a monopoly public utility to a company that had to change its corporate culture to compete in the open market (Shafritz et al., p. 394).

Joseph was a transformational leader. After he interpreted Pharaoh's dreams; he advised him to choose a wise man and put him in charge of the land of Egypt. "Let Pharaoh appoint commissioners over the land to take a fifth of the harvest of Egypt during the seven years of abundance. They should collect all the food of these good years that are coming and store up the grain under the authority of Pharaoh, to be kept in the cities for food. This food should be held in reserve for the country, to be used during the seven years of famine that will come upon Egypt, so that the country may not be ruined by the famine" (Genesis 41: 34-36). Joseph, who was also a visionary leader, gave the plan to administer the country in a period of abundance and famine. A transformational leader is also a visionary leader who thinks about what can happen in the future and prepare to avoid it as the American's government always does. When an incident occurs in the United States, the government and university experts analyze why that incident has occurred and ponder how to avoid it again. For example, there was no Homeland Security Department before September 11, 2001. Still, to prevent another terrorist attack and protect the United States' interests worldwide, President George W. Bush has created a special department known Homeland Security Department. Pharaoh, as a democrat leader, did not waste time to choose the right person: Joseph. We sometimes fail because we do not use the right leader to collaborate with us. "The plan seemed good to Pharaoh and to all his officials. So, Pharaoh asked them, 'can we find anyone like this man, one in whom is the spirit of God?'" (Genesis 41: 37). I should analyze an essential point in Pharaoh's question; he did not make any decisions without questioning all officials of his government. 'Can we find anyone like this man, one in whom is the spirit of God?'; he knew clearly there is no one like Joseph in Egypt because when he had the dream ' in the morning his mind was troubled, so he sent for all the magicians and wise men of Egypt. Pharaoh told them his dreams, but no one could interpret them for him' (Genesis 41: 8). That is the real trait of a great leader! A great leader never wastes time to take a final decision when all elements seem clear. Who is like Joseph? No one! If they wanted to protect the country, who should have chosen to administer Egypt? Joseph! The wise man; the man who was qualified or had skills for that position. An administration should have the right administrators to be efficient.

Then Pharaoh said to Joseph, 'Since God has made all this known to you, there is no one so discerning and wise as you. You shall be in charge of my palace, and all my people are to submit to your orders. Only with respect to the throne will I be greater than you (Genesis 41: 39-40). Pharaoh did not care about Joseph's nationality. He immediately changed Joseph's name and gave him an Egyptian's name. "So Pharaoh said to Joseph, 'I hereby put you in charge of the whole land of Egypt.' 'Then Pharaoh took his signet ring from his finger and put it on Joseph's finger' (Genesis 41: 41,2). The ring symbolized the alliance between Joseph who became Egyptian by naturalization. "He dressed him in robes of fine linen and put a gold chain around his neck. He had him ride in a chariot as his second-in-command, and men shouted before him, 'Make way!' Thus he put him in charge of the whole land of Egypt. Then Pharaoh said to Joseph, 'I am Pharaoh, but without your word no one will lift hand or foot in all Egypt.' Pharaoh gave Joseph the name Zaphenath-Paneah and gave him Asenath daughter of Potiphera, priest of On, to be his wife. And Joseph went throughout the land of Egypt" (Genesis 41: 42-45).

A transformational leader does not see only his/her interest but the interests of others. It does not take time to see a transformational leader; since his/her first day of administration, all his/her collaborators would determine that this guy is a transformational leader. Some leaders think they should talk all the time or be present to be a transformational or a visionary leader; I do not think so. A great leader never talks too much and is never present all the time when it is not necessary because he/she should give access to subaltern leaders to execute his/her order. Most of the time, leaders who talk a lot and are always present are not transformational or visionary leaders. Leaders, who get great staff, do not have to make an appearance all the time; but they should give their collaborators access to implement their policies. You would never see a United States President or a President of a developed country make an appearance to the public all the time; he makes an appearance to the public when there is a national disaster or when the country's interest is clearly in danger.

Jesus was also a transformational and visionary leader. He was born in a formalism society where the political and religious leaders said to people what to do, and they did not observe those laws. 'Anyone who breaks one of the least of these commandments and teaches others to do the same will be called least in the kingdom of heaven, but whoever practices and teaches these commands will be called great in heaven's kingdom. For I tell you that unless your righteousness surpasses that of the Pharisees and the teachers of the law, you will certainly not enter the kingdom of heaven' (Matthew 5: 19-20). He has reviewed all Judaism's laws. About murder, he argues that you have heard that it was said to the people long ago, 'Do not murder, and anyone who murders will be subject to judgment.' But I tell you that anyone who is angry with his brother will be subject to judgment" (Matthew 5: 21-22). About adultery, he asserts that you have heard that it was said, do not commit adultery. But I tell you that anyone who looks at a woman lustfully has already committed adultery with her in his heart (Matthew 5: 27). Then if fixing a woman with a desire is a sin, anyone can be adultery. The following statements would help you understand the change that He has made about adultery: But went to the Mount of Olives. At dawn he appeared again in the temple courts, where all the people gathered around him, and he sat down to teach them. The teachers of the law and the Pharisees brought in a woman caught in adultery. They made her stand before the group and said to Jesus, 'Teacher, this woman was caught in the act of adultery. In the Law Moses commanded us to stone such Woman. Now what do you say? They were using this question as a trap, in order to have a basis for accusing him. But Jesus bent down and started to write on the ground with his finger. When they kept on questioning him, he straightened up and said to them, 'If anyone of you is without sin, let him be the first to throw a stone at her.' Again, he stooped down and wrote on the ground. At this, those who heard began to go away one at a time, the older ones first, until only Jesus was left, with the Woman still standing there. Jesus straightened up and asked her, 'Woman, where are they? Has no one condemned you? 'No one, sir,' she said. 'Then neither do I condemn you,' Jesus declared. 'Go now and leave your life of sin' (John 8: 1-11). That scene tells you clearly that Jesus was/is a transformational leader. In the Beatitudes, He taught His disciples about the main issues that provoked problems in Judaism's society, such as murder, adultery, divorce, oaths, an Eye for an Eye, love for enemies, charity, prayer, fasting, the kingdom of heaven, and judging others.

No one can change a society without knowing its primary problem and reviewing its common law. Jesus, by His teachings, changed the community partially during His lifetime. His disciples had continued to teach His philosophy after the ascension. His philosophy does not bring change in a region but worldwide. His philosophy continued to lead by His disciples or followers to change the world. Then Jesus is a tremendous transformational and visionary leader.

a. *Too much leadership*

Structural rigidity often causes managers to overmanage—to lead too much. *Micromanage* is the pejorative term for supervising too closely. Any manager may be guilty of micromanagement for refusing to allow subordinates to have any real authority or responsibility, thereby ensuring that subordinates can neither function as nor grow into effective managers. Furthermore, the managers are kept so busy micromanaging that they never have time to do what managers are supposed to do—like develop a long-term strategy and overall vision (Shafritz et al., p. 395). Most of the time, leaders with low self-esteem do not accept collaborating with others; they apparently can share their position with others to use them as dummy or photo. In Haitian culture, they usually use word photos or portraits to identify someone who occupies a job and does not do anything, but they see him/her while someone else does what he or she is supposed to do. We can identify this theory as a photo/portrait or dummy theory. We might find that concept everywhere, such as churches, private and public organizations. Some leaders sometimes choose weak leaders as subalterns to control them as they want to for their purpose—this mentality develops in developing countries where there is corruption. Public administrators could have many non-existing names in the payroll list; they call this list a zombie list or check zombie. Those employees are never on duty, but they always have their paychecks. Leaders who exercise too much leadership never trust their collaborator; they pretend they are the only person that can do everything. Most of the time, those leaders talk a lot; they always be present to solve any little problem; they still have the last word. If there are not present, their organization cannot function. They are arrogant, and they do not have respect for anyone.

b. Moses Leadership

Moses was a great leader, even though he did not know that he could exercise leadership. He was born leader; he had trained for forty years in the palace and forty years in Midian wilderness, where he encountered Zipporah, daughter of Jethro, also called Reuel. God called him while he was in Midian Wilderness to deliver His people in Egypt, but he did not accept that task that God gives him even God identifies who he is to Moses "… I am the God of thy father, the God of Abraham, the God of Isaac, and Jacob God. And Moses hid his face; for he was afraid to look upon God. The Lord said, I have surely seen the affliction of my people which are in Egypt and have heard their cry because of their taskmasters; for I know their sorrows. And I am come down to deliver them out of the hand of the Egyptians, and to bring them up out of that land flowing with milk and honey; unto the place of the Canaanites, and the Hittites, and the Amorites, and the Perizzites, and the Hivites, and Jebusites. Now therefore, behold, the cry of the children of Israel has come unto me: and I have also seen the oppression wherewith the Egyptians oppress them. Come now, therefore, and I will send thee unto Pharaoh, that thou mayest bring forth my people the children of Israel out of Egypt. And Moses said unto God, who am I, that I should go unto Pharaoh, and that I should bring forth the children of Israel out of Egypt? (Exodus 3:6-11).

After an extended dialogue between God and Moses, Moses would have accepted His order. After Pharaoh let them go, it looks like he was the only one decision-maker that made his task more difficult. Moses' leadership is authoritarian; an authoritarian leader cannot be a democrat. He does whatever he wants to, and he is the only one to decide. Most of the time, autocratic leaders are dictators; they rule in magister dixit like elementary teachers to their students. Moses was Dixit authoritarian not because he wanted to, but he would like to observe word by word God terms.

He was a leader who cared about his duty. He was like a manager who has received the order from the CEO of an organization and does not want to hire anyone to execute it because he wants the job to be well done.

c. Jethro Leadership (Exode 18:14-21)

Shafritz et al. (2009) consider Jethro as the first Moses Management Consultant. They assert that Moses, while certainly an effective and charismatic leader, could not delegate. "The system" he created would not let him let go. He had thousands of people reporting to him. The managerial workload became overwhelming. The ancient Israelites by the hundreds were unhappily standing in line "from the morning unto the evening" to confer with him. Finally, Jethro, Moses' father-in-law, became the first-known management consultant when he gave Moses the reengineering advice he needed to create a more competent organization. First, he assessed the problem: And Moses' father-in-law said, "The thing that thou doest is not good. Thou wilt surely wear away, both thou, and this people that is with thee: for this thing is too heavy for thee: thou art not able to perform it thyself alone. Hearken now unto my voice, and I will give thee counsel. Thou shalt teach them ordinances and laws, and shalt show them how they must walk (Shafritz et al., p. 223).

Who was Jethro?

Now Moses Kept the flock of Jethro his father in law, the priest of Midian: and he led the flock to the backside of the desert, and came to the mountain of God, even to Hored (Exodus 3: 1). According to Halley commentary, Jethro, as a priest of Midian, must have been a ruler. Midianites were descended from Abraham through

Keturah (Genesis 25:2) (p. 120). As a ruler, Jethro has experienced a power-sharing model for leading the Midian people; then, he knows the effectiveness of power-sharing. Consequently, he can share that experience with Moses, his son in law that many have considered a charismatic leader. Can one consider Moses as an authoritarian leader? No! If Moses were an authoritarian leader, he would never accept and apply his father's advice in law, Jethro. Moses was not on his own; he was controlled by God and wanted to follow God's path. He led Israel under the Theocracy power; he was a moral leader who knew his accountability and fought to respect his accountability until God determines that his job is over because the people of Israel drove him crazy in the desert and pushed him to take a wrong decision. God tells him to speak to the rock, but Moses struck the rock twice instead of speaking to the rock (Numbers 20: 9-11).

d. Power-sharing

Our conception of the shared-power world began developing in the early 1980s and was influenced considerably by a 1984 Humphrey Institute conference on shared power, inspired by Harlan Cleveland and organized by John Bryson and Robert Einsweiler (see Bryson and Einsweiler, 1991, for selected conference presentations). The conference theme reflected an atmosphere of disillusionment with the grand U.S. government schemes of the 1960s and growing recognition of global interdependence and complexity. Old notions of leaders who were in charge of situations, organizations, and even nations seemed not to apply (Crosby, P. 17). There is nothing new under the sun, said Solomon (Ecclesiastes 1:9); the power-sharing system existed since the existence of the universe. God (Elohim) remains a symbol of power-sharing. There is one God in three persons: Father, Son, and Holy Spirit; all of them have powers, but in each dispensation, we have seen the manifestation of one of them. In the period vetero-testamentary, the Son and the Holy Spirit were not on duty, but only God the Father was on duty, but it does not mean that God (Father) did not use them. That power-sharing is stable and cannot be destroyed because all actors are the same interests. However, sometimes fake power-sharing is power-sharing to calm the enemy and destroy it like Jacob's sons did to Shechem and his dad. Shechem loved Dinah, the daughter of Jacob, and violated her. Hamor, the Hivite, the ruler of that area, negotiated with Jacob and his sons. My son Shechem has his heart set on your daughter. Please give her to him as his wife. Intermarry with us; give us your daughters and take our daughters for yourselves. You can settle among us; the land is open to you. Live in it, trade in it, and acquire property in it. Then Shechem said to Dinah's father and brothers, let me find favor in your eyes, and I will give you whatever you ask. Make the bride's price and the gift I am to bring as great as you like, and I'll pay whatever you ask me. Only give me the girl as my wife. Because their sister Dinah had been defiled, Jacob's sons replied deceitfully as they spoke to Shechem and his father Hamor. They said to them, 'we can't do such a thing; we can't give our sister to a man who is not circumcised. That would be a disgrace to us. We will give our consent to you on one condition only: that you become like us by circumcising all your males. Then we will give you our daughters and take your daughters for ourselves. We'll settle among you and become one people with you. But if you will not agree to be circumcised, we'll take our sister and go. ... Three days later, while all of them were still in pain, two of Jacob's sons, Simeon and Levi, Dinah's brothers, took their swords and attacked the unsuspecting city, killing every male (Genesis 34: 8- 25). A weak party usually may be destroyed by the strongest party. Dinah's brothers attacked Hivite when all men are in pain and cannot fight.

David and Saul, the first king of Israel, were another style of power-sharing. After defeated Goliath, he became a member of Saul's family; Jonathan, Saul's son, became his best friend. Even though Saul did not like David because he became more popular than him, but he still wants David to be in his government. Saul said to David, here is my older daughter Merab. I will give her to you in marriage; only serve me bravely and fight the battles of the Lord. For Saul said to himself, I will not raise a hand against him. Let the Philistines do that! But David said to Saul, who am I, and what is my family or my father's clan in Israel, that I should become the king's son-in-law? So, when the time came for Merab, Saul's daughter, to be given to David, she was given in marriage to Adriel of Meholah. Now Saul's daughter Michal was in love with David, and when they told Saul about it, he was pleased. I will give her to him, he thought, so that she may be a snare to him and so that the hand of the Philistines may be against him. So, Saul said to David, Now you have a second opportunity to become my son-in-law. (I Samuel 18: 17-21). One considers that power-sharing as more dangerous living in your enemy's house, someone who is jealous of you.

Viewed another way, shared-power arrangements exist in the midrange of a continuum of how organizations work on public problems. At one end of the continuum are organizations that hardly relate to each other or are adversaries, dealing with a prob- lem that extends beyond their capabilities. At the other end are or- ganizations merged into a new entity that can handle the problem through merged authority and capabilities. In the midrange are organizations that share information, undertake joint projects, or develop shared-power arrangements such as collaborations or coalitions (see also Himmelman, 1996) (Crosby, p. 18). Two organizations can also be merged to serve the public more efficiently, which is also another kind of power-sharing. Those organizations put together all their materials and human resources to become stronger.

Power-sharing remains the best method to solve any conflict, whatever its origin because power is the leading cause of war. It could define as a bilateral or multilateral compromising to end a war. For example, Nelson Mandella remains a great charismatic leader; F.W. de Klerk, the former President of South Africa, after the international pressure, accepted to abolish the apartheid system in 1990. "In April 1994 the Mandela-led ANC won South Africa's first elections by universal suffrage, and on May 10 Mandela was sworn in as president of the country's first multiethnic government. He established in 1995 the Truth and Reconciliation Commission (TRC), which investigated human rights violations under apartheid, and he introduced housing, standards of the country's black population. In 1996 he oversaw the enactment of a new transferring leadership of the party to his designated successor, Thabo Mbeki. Mandela and Madikizela-Mandela had divorced in 1996, and in 1998 Mandela married Graca Machel, the widow of Samora Machel, the former Mozambican president and leader of Frelimo" (http://www.britannica.com/EBchecked/topic/361645/Nelson-Mandela/282997/Presidency-and-retirement). According to Ramsbotham et al. (2010), the structure of the conflict lay in the incompatibility between the National Party (NP) government which was determined to uphold white power and privileges through the apartheid system, and the black majority which sought radical change and a non-racial, equal society based on one-person-one-vote. Transforming this conflict involved first the empowerment of the majority through political mobilization and the campaign of resistance against the apartheid laws. The revolt in the townships, political mobilization and movements like Steve Biko's 'Black Consciousness' all expressed the refusal of the majority to acquiesce in a racially dominated society. Externally, the international pressure on the South African regime partly offset the internal imbalance of power, through the anti-apartheid campaign, international isolation, sporting bans, partial sanctions and disinvestment (p.177). The international pressure on South Africa was beneficial; South Africa was isolated from the world. It could not involve any world activities, even trading. Then the international pressure affected the economy of the country altogether; as a result, the minority group that kept the majority of the population who are black in captivity in their soil decided to change the apartheid system allowing all ethnic groups to be equal and could involve in all social activities in the country. A turning-point came in 1989-90. De Klerk shifted decisively towards a policy of negotiations: he began to end segregation, lifted the ban on the ANC, and finally released Mandela on 11 February 1990. By the Groote Schuur Minute of May 1990, the government agreed to 'work toward lifting the state of emergency', while the ANC agreed to 'curb violence'. The ANC had now accepted that the NP would remain in power while negotiations were carried out, and the NP that it would have to give up its monopoly of power. The government's aim was now a power-sharing agreement, in which its future role in a multiracial government would be guaranteed (Ramsbotham et al, p. 179). The decision of De Klerk to end segregation remains a great decision, and De Klerk should be considered as a great leader. People usually talk about Mandela leadership which is not bad, but also, we should consider De Klerk as a great leader. He has decided to make compromised instead of resisting because he loved his country. Also, without any complex, he has decided to collaborate in Mandela's government. Most developing countries leaders would never accept that deal. The power sharing of South Africa could be considered as the most efficient power sharing in the modern world. The minority leaders of that country did not think about their power, but they think about political stability of their country. All developing countries leaders should take South Africa as an example. Even though the internal conflict of developing countries is different than South Africa conflict, but there is one and only one way that an internal conflict can be solved is power sharing because power is the main cause of all conflicts in developing countries.

The Rwanda conflict in 1994 is another example. Ethnic violence, therefore, was a two-way street. Although the Hutu government was undoubtedly responsible for much of the recent violence, both sides had bloody hands. The only way to end the civil war and break the cycle of ethnic violence was to establish a political process that secured a cease-fire and led to a multiethnic government that enshrined democratic practices. This was the raison d'être of the Arusha Accords (Barnett, p.113). Rwanda's genocide remains crueler than any genocide than has occurred in the world. People from the same country, who have the same culture and socialize daily to each other, become enemies to kill each other due to ethnic issues. Tutsi, a minority ethnic group, let Belgian washed their brain to let them know they look Europeans, and Hutu, a majority ethnic group declared war against Tutsi. Hutu's students didn't care about their Tutsi's professors; Hutu's neighbors didn't care about Tutsi's neighbors' life. Hutu didn't care even about little children's life. They have killed many people. People from the same country kill each other! That is so sad! However, all antagonists had accepted to make a compromise by forming a multiethnic government allowing the inhabitants' lifestyle to become normal. It could be hard for both ethnic groups to collaborate when they remember the loved one they have lost during that conflict; however, they would agree to deal with each other to end the conflict and allow their country to function normally.

e. *Charismatic leadership*

The Charismatic Leader gathers followers through dint of personality and charm, rather than any form of external power or authority. It is interesting to watch a Charismatic Leader 'working the room' as they move from person to person. They pay much attention to the person they are talking to at any one moment, making that person feel like they are, for that time, the most important person in the world. Charismatic Leaders pay a great deal of attention in scanning and reading their environment and are good at picking up the moods and concerns of both individuals and larger audiences. They then will hone their actions and words to suit the situation. Pulling all of the strings Charismatic Leaders use a wide range of methods to manage their image and, if they are not naturally charismatic, may practice assiduously at developing their skills. They may engender trust through visible self-sacrifice and taking personal risks in the name of their beliefs. They will show great confidence in their followers. They are very persuasive and make very effective use of body language as well as verbal language. Deliberate charisma is played out in a theatrical sense, where the leader is 'playing to the house' to create a desired effect. They also make effective use of storytelling, including the use of symbolism and metaphor. Many politicians use a charismatic style, as they need to gather a large number of followers. If you want to increase your charisma, studying videos of their speeches and the way they interact with others is a great source of learning. Religious leaders, too, may well use charisma, as do cult leaders) (http://www.rose-hulman.edu/StudentAffairs/ra/files/CLSK/PDF/). A Charismatic leader may be considered as a leader who knows the exact words to motivate, manipulate, and persuade people to believe what they don't believe before, and to do what they do not do before. Is it a great character? Yes! Charismatic leaders usually help people to recognize their rights and fight for it. Their traits remain a gift - receiving from God; it is an ability they have that does not depend on their educational background. It is an innate character. They always find words easily for any circumstances to convince people. With Logos they have power to control people's brain to do what they want to even miracles. The world has been created with logos. "God said, 'Let there be light,' and there was light. ... God said, 'Let there be an expanse between the waters to separate water from water.' ... And God said, 'Let the water under the sky be gathered to one place, and let dry ground appear.'... Then God said, 'Let the land produce vegetation: seed-bearing plants and trees on the land that bear fruit with seed in it, according to their various kinds.' And God said, 'Let there be lights in the expanse of the sky to separate the day from the night, and let them serve as signs to mark seasons and days and years, and let them be lights in the expanse of the sky to give light on the earth.' ...And God said, 'Let the water teem with living creatures, and let birds fly above the earth across the expanse of the sky.'... And God said, 'Let the land produce living creatures according to their kinds: livestock, creatures that move along the ground, and wild animals, each according to its kind.' ...Then God said, 'Let us make man in our image, in our likeness, and let them rule over the fish of the sea and the birds of the air, over the livestock, over all the earth, and over all the creatures that move along the ground' (Genesis 1).

Power is logos because logos is power. The scripture teaches us that in the beginning was the Word, and the Word was with God, and the Word was God. He was with God in the beginning. Through him all things were made; without him nothing was made that has been made (John 1: 1-3). Jesus, who was a charismatic leader, made many miracles by logos. "When Jesus had entered Capernaum, a centurion came to him, asking for help. Lord, he said, 'my servant lies at home paralyzed and in terrible suffering.' Jesus said to him, 'I will go and heal him.' The centurion replied, 'Lord, I do not deserve to have you come under my roof. But just say the word, and my servant will be healed. For I myself am a man under authority, with soldiers under me. I tell this one, 'Go,' and he goes; and that one, 'Come,' and he comes. I say to my servant, 'Do this,' and he does it.' When Jesus heard this, he was astonished and said to those following him, 'I tell you the truth, I have not found anyone in Israel with such great faith. I say to you that many will come from the east and the west and will take their places at the feast with Abraham, Isaac and Jacob in the kingdom of heaven. But the subjects of the kingdom will be thrown outside, into the darkness, where there will be weeping and gnashing of teeth.' Then Jesus said to the centurion, 'Go! It will be done just as you believed it would.' And his servant was healed at that very hour (Matthew 8: 5-13). The centurion had faith in Jesus' word; he believed that his word is so powerful to heal his servant.

Another great miracle that Jesus has made with the word was the Jairus' daughter, who was declared dead. "While Jesus was still speaking, some men came from the house of Jairus, the synagogue ruler. 'Your daughter is dead,' they said. 'Why bother the teacher anymore?' Ignoring what they said, Jesus told the synagogue ruler, 'Don't be afraid; just believe.' He did not let anyone follow him except Peter, James and John the brother of James. When they came to the home of the synagogue ruler, Jesus saw a commotion, with people crying and wailing loudly. He went in and said to them, 'Why all this commotion and wailing? The child is not dead but asleep.' But they laughed at him. After he put them all out, he took the child's father and mother and the disciples who were with him and went in where the child was. He took her by the hand and said to her, 'Talitha koum!' (which means, 'Little girl, I say to you, get up!'). Immediately the girl stood up and walked around (she was twelve years old). At this they were completely astonished (Mark 5: 35-42). There is an important thing to remember in Jesus 'conversation about the death of Jairus' daughter. 'Don't be afraid; just believe.' When you believe in someone you cannot be afraid when he is present; you always think he can do something that people would not expect. It is precisely the characteristic of a charismatic leader, giving hope to people and letting them know that the situation can be changed and prove how it can be changed. A real charismatic leader would not talk without proving the reality of his words.

Martin Luther King Jr. was a charismatic leader; he believed that the situation of Black-American could be changed a day. He even prophesized about how the relation between Black and White Americans would be. In his famous speech, ' I have a Dream', you can see his determination and reality. In our generation, we can argue that the King's dream becomes a reality. Even though racism is not over, but today black and white can join each other. There are no segregation schools and no segregation transportation system. Most of the United States people have elected President Barack Hussein Obama as the first black-American to lead the United States during two terms. Many black officials (Black Caucus) in American government work with their white colleagues to make the United States a better place on earth for people to live.

Father Gerard Jean Juste was also a charismatic leader; he fought against the United States Immigration Services, allowing Haitian refugees to become legal in the United States. My parents were illegal immigrants; if I can live in the United States today and have a high education level, I should thank Father Jean Juste 'Gerry', who is not alive today. They have killed him because they knew that he would continue to fight to change Haitian people's life if he became President of Haiti. They had accused him of being a criminal; he was arrested and in prison in Haiti; while he was in jail, they mistreated him and empoisoned his blood. He was dead with leukemia in Miami, Florida, where he fought for Haitian refugee and Haiti freedom. He was a supporter of former President Jean Bertrand Aristide, who is a charismatic leader.

3. Moral Leadership

Political scientist Garry Wills in the *Atlantic Monthly* warns that "if the leader is just an expediter of what other people want, a resource for their use, the people are not being *led* but *serviced*." Thus it is moving people in new directions—taking them to places where they did not know they wanted or needed to go— that is the essence of leadership and has been since ancient times. Thucydides, in his *History of the Peloponnesian War*, describes Pericles, the leader of ancient Athens, as someone who, because he was so "clearly above corruption, was enabled, by the respect others had for him and his own wise policy, to hold the multitude in a voluntary restraint." Thus "he led them, not they him; and since he did not win his power on compromising terms, he could say not only what pleased others but what displeased them, relying on their respect."(Shafritz et al., p. 397).

Pericles exercised moral leadership. He was able to send people in new directions of action and thought because it was the right and decent thing to do. During the presidential campaign of 1932, then New York Governor Franklin D. Roosevelt spoke for all political executives when he said, "The presidency is not merely an administrative office. That's the least of it. It is more than an engineering job, efficient or inefficient. It is preeminently a place of moral leadership. All our great presidents were leaders of thought at times when certain historic ideas in the life of the nation had to be clarified." Presidents have traditionally used what President Theodore Roosevelt called their "bully (meaning "first-rate") pulpit" to provide this clarification. (Shafritz et al, p. 397). There is only one institution that teaches the real morality, and where one finds moral leadership is the Christian church. A Christian who becomes president of a country will exercise moral leadership because the bible already taught him/her what morality is.

4. Democratic Leadership

Democracy meaning participative management works (Shafritz et al., p. 391). People from developing countries always misunderstand 'democracy'; for them, democracy means freedom to do whatever they want, even if it can hurt others. Democracy without laws of regulations is not democracy is anarchy. Then an organization where people do whatever they want without thinking about any regulations cannot make progress; it is an anarchic organization. An anarchic organization's outcome is destruction, division, violence, lack of ethics, and progress. A democratic leader allows everyone to participate in public affairs or community development while respecting each other rights.

In the 1980s and 1990s, across the world, democratic movements have contributed to promoting human rights, liberty, freedom, and democracy in developing countries. Democratic movements have accounted for the historical progress of democracy (Minier, 2001). In some countries, citizens have fought against dictatorship, military regimes, and racial segregation. They have subverted autocratic and military governments and contributed to the establishment of new democratic governments and institutions. The power of citizens has been the key factor in promoting democratically social changes and democratic systems (Fox & Brown, 2000; Wiseman, 1996). Leaders in democratic movements have organized the power of citizens and have struggled for democracy (http://www.regent.edu/acad/global/publications/ijls/new/vol2iss3/choi/Choi_Vol2Iss3.pdf).

King David gives us a great example of democracy while attempting to move the Ark that had been taken by the Philistines at the battle of Ebenezer (I Sam. 5); he consulted with the captains of thousands and hundreds, and with every leader. Moreover, David said unto all the congregation of Israel, If it seems good unto you, and that it be of the Lord our God, let us send abroad unto our brethren everywhere, that are left in all the land of Israel, and with them also to the priests and Levites which are in their cities and suburbs, that they may gather themselves unto us. And let us bring the ark of our God again to us: for we enquired not at it in the days of Saul. The whole assembly agreed to do this because it seemed right to all the people (I Chronicles 13: 1-4).

Jehoshaphat's behavior also is an example of democratic leadership; he had learned that many peoples plotted to invade Judah. "… And Jehoshaphat feared, and set himself to seek the Lord, and proclaimed a fast throughout all Judah. And Judah gathered themselves together, to ask help of the Lord: even out of all the cities of Judah they came to seek the Lord" (II Chronicles 20: 3,4). Then he invited his people to seek the Lord together and find an outcome together.

5. Team Leadership

A team might begin as an informal working group and progress to a more formal arrangement, examples being a task force, steering committee, planning team, or standing committee. They may come together for a relatively brief period of time to complete a specific task, or they may last for years (although the membership might change) (Crosby, p. 64). Nehemiah's mission to rebuild the wall of Jerusalem is an example of 'Team Leadership'; he mobilized and encouraged Judah's fellow citizens to gather and rebuild the wall. "Then said I unto them, Ye see the distress that we are in, how Jerusalem lieth waste and the gates thereof are burned with fire: come, and let us build up the wall of Jerusalem, that we be no more a reproach"(Nehemiah 2: 17).

6. Organizational Leadership

Advocates of major policy change must ensure that effective and humane organizations are created, maintained, or restructured as needed (Crosby, p.77). That is exactly what Nehemiah did advocating to rebuild the wall of Jerusalem while "Sanballat and his allies had adopted a hostile attitude to the Jews when he originally heard of their intention to rebuild Jerusalem's wall (2:19). On hearing now that this intention was being implemented his hostility towards them increased, and he ridiculed the Jews, calling them feeble, and mocking their procedure of using as materials for the new wall stones from the old wall, and burned ones at that, which might well be cracked and weak. The taunt of Tobiah was that so flimsy was this restored wall that a mere fox touching it would have enough impact to knock it down. The Jews, however, were not deterred by these jibes, and instead of answering back or retaliating they committed the matter to God in prayer and continued with the building. Because of this, Sanballat decided now to resort to physical attacks. For this purpose, he gathered his allies, adding to his former ones (2:19) the men of Ashdod, the ancient Philistine country to Jerusalem's west. The Jews had enemies now to the north (Sanballat in Samaria), to the south (Geshem the Arab), and the west (the Ashdodites). Sanballat, their leader, could not formally declare war on the Jews, for Samaria and Judah both belonged to the Persian empire and were subject to Artaxerxes who had specifically authorized the rebuilding of Jerusalem's wall. But the enemies felt themselves able to engage themselves in sporadic terrorist activities against the Jews. Again Nehemiah prayed about the matter, and he exhorted his people to place their trust in God's invincible power which He could exercise on their behalf" (Short, p. 501).

Nehemiah chapter 4 teaches us all strategies of those who oppose rebuilding Jerusalem's wall and Jews' systems to continue their task without thinking about their enemy plotting. But it came to pass, that when Sanballat heard that we builded the wall, he was wroth, and took great indignation, and mocked the Jews. And he spake before his brethren and the army of Samaria, and said, what do these feeble Jews? Will they fortify themselves? Will they sacrifice? Will they make an end in a day? Will they revive the stones out of the heaps of the rubbish which are burned? Now Tobiah the Ammonite was by him, and he said, Even that which they build if a fox goes up, he shall even break down their stone wall. Hear, O our God; for we are despised: and turn their reproach upon their own head, and give them for a prey in the land of captivity: And cover not their iniquity, and let not their sin be blotted out from before thee: for they have provoked thee to anger before the builders. So built we the wall; and all the wall was joined together unto the half thereof: for the people had a mind to work. But it came to pass, that when Sanballat, and Tobiah, and the Arabians, and the Ammonites, and the Ashdodites, heard that the walls of Jerusalem were made up, and that the breaches began to be stopped, then they were very wroth, and conspired all of them together to come and to fight against Jerusalem, and to hinder it. Nevertheless we made our prayer unto our God, and set a watch against them day and night, because of them. And Judah said, The strength of the bearers of burdens is decayed, and there is much rubbish; so that we are not able to build the wall. And our adversaries said, They shall not know, neither see, till we come in the midst among them, and slay them, and cause the work to cease. And it came to pass, that when the Jews which dwelt by them came, they said unto us ten times, From all places whence ye shall return unto us they will be upon you. Therefore, I set I in the lower places behind the wall, and on the higher places, I even set the people after their families with their swords, spears, and bows. Furthermore, I looked, and rose up, and said unto the nobbles, and to the rulers, and to the rest of the people, Be not ye afraid of them: remember the Lord, which is great and terrible, and fight for your brethren, your sons, and your daughters, your wives, and your houses. And it came to pass when our enemies heard that it was known unto us, and God had brought their counsel to naught, that we returned all of us to the wall, everyone unto his work. And it came to pass from that time forth, that the half of my servants wrought in the work, and the other half of them held both the spears, the shields, and the bows, and the habergeons; and the rulers were behind all the house of Judah. They which built on the wall, and they that bare burdens, with those that laded, everyone with one of his hands wrought in work, and with the other hand held a weapon. For the builders, everyone had his sword girded by his side, and so built. And he that sounded the trumpet was by me.

7. Visionary Leadership

Visionary leadership shapes the meaning of public problems and inspires commitment to proposed solutions. Political leadership achieves adoption and implementation of policies, programs, and projects incorporating the solutions. Ethical leadership helps settle disputes over those policies, programs, and projects, and it sanctions conduct (Crosby,p. 108).

Visionary leaders create and communicate meaning about historical events, current reality, group mission, and prospects for the future.(Crosby,p. 109). At least two significant events occurred in the 21st century; they might focus on the terrorist attacks on September 11, 2001, and the Katrina disaster. The local and federal government behavior vis-à-vis 9/11 terrorists attacks and Katrina disaster remain very different; the 9/11 terrorist attacks showed clearly the determination of local authority to serve their country and know their accountability. The New York firefighters did not stop running into the flames to save lives even they knew that their own life is in jeopardy. According to Shafritz et al. (2009), Mayblum is only one of thousands who fled down the stairs to safety from the inferno of the World Trade Center towers as firefighters and other rescue workers raced up the stairs into deadly danger. The essence of the firefighters' bravery can be summed up by an old observation: Firefighters don't run from burning buildings; they run into them (p.2). Those firefighters knew their role; they knew that they should accomplish their public service mission. Shafritz et al. (2009) compare them as Spartans; they assert that the similarities between the New York City firefighters and the Spartans of ancient Greece go far beyond the number 300. And that number is not accurate in either case. The 343 firefighters who died were in the company of 136 other rescue workers (New York City Police, (Port Authority Police, Private security guards, etc.) who also died. The Spartans had auxiliaries (somebody had to cook) and small combat units from other cities, including about 1,000 Thespians (not actors, but soldiers from Thespiae). Nevertheless, the number 300 resonates because it was the Spartans who fought to the death while others retreated (p.2). Those firefighters should be honored.

President Bush did not cross his hands after 9/11; he said : " While the U.S. will constantly strive to enlist the support of the international community, we [Americans] will not hesitate to act alone, if necessary, to exercise our right of self-defense by acting preemptively against such terrorists, to prevent them from doing harm against our people and our country; and denying further sponsorship, support, and sanctuary to terrorists by convincing or compelling states to accept their sovereign responsibilities" (Goldstein et al. 2006, p.96). He fought the terrorist to revenge 9/11.

President Bush's behavior and all firefighters mean a lot for public administration today; we see in those firefighters real public servants who are not hesitated to jeopardize their life to respect their job's ethics. In President Bush, we see an authoritarian leader who decides whatever what other allies or countries think about his action; he is also a visionary leader. His country is in danger while he is the commander in chief; he has decided to secure his country by declaring war on terror. It is the main reason that President Bush has created a new department to defend United States soil, its allied, and its interest, which is the Homeland Security Department. This act of President Bush could be considered as 'Redefining public service'. 9/11 terrorist attacks remain a critical issue of public service in the 21st century; many experts have questioned this attack on how enemies of the United States could attack the United States soil while the intelligence services did not know this attack and avoid it. Suppose they knew it, according to many experts or observers, why the intelligence service would not stop this attack. Even though terrorist attacks have occurred, but the Bush administration did a great job defending the United States soil and its allies.

However, the local and federal governments did not pay too much attention to the Katrina disaster; it looks like that event did not occur in the United States. No authority intervenes before the disaster to avoid it and after to support those who are in need. Most scholars refer to bureaucrat bashing to explaining the behavior of the local and federal government. According to Shafritz et al. (2009), bashing is extreme and public criticism of a person, policy, or nation. Domestically, bashing has often followed the word bureaucrat. During the 1980s, the constant complaints and jokes about the competence of government employees – led by President Ronald "Government Is the Problem" Reagan – helped to create an acceptance of bureaucrat bashing (p.284). Yet, when Katrina hit land (Stillman II, 2010), during the first fifteen hours of August 29, 2005, the levee system failed. Seven hundred and fifty thousand people in New Orleans were left homeless, nearly 1,000 died, 100,000 homes were underwater, numerous businesses and public institutions were destroyed, with losses estimated in the hundreds of billions of dollars, resulting in the worst natural disaster in American history (p.226).

If the local government of New York and the federal government should be honored for their behavior during 9/11, the local government of New Orleans and the federal government should not be honored for their behavior after the Katrina disaster. This event means a lot for public administration because the local and federal administration did not intervene to rescue despaired people in Louisiana. The public administration's future in Louisiana should take a lesson of Katrina, avoiding another disaster in the future. Those two issues have an immense impact on public administration; 9/11 has a positive impact, and the Katrina disaster has a negative impact. Public administration scholars and academics should encourage public administrators to copy those firefighters who died on duty because they knew their responsibility; however, both the local government, even the federal government, both failed to accomplish their mission, which is protecting and serving their population. Public administration scholars should also encourage public administrators from all sectors to respect their engagement, vis-à-vis their population. They should scrutinize the behavior of those administrators vis-à-vis the Louisiana population to determine the causes of that disaster.

V

Organizational Development

ORGANIZATION DEVELOPMENT (OD) IS PLANNED organizational change. Organizations exist in a dynamic environment, both internally and externally, to which they must respond or become ineffectual. The responsibility of OD advisers, specialists on applied behavioral science, is to facilitate change—to use their knowledge of the behavioral sciences for organizational improvement. These advisers can be internal in that they already work for the organization or external independent consultants. A frequently desired change is the installation of a beneficent managerial philosophy. More modest goals might be the creation of an atmosphere of trust in order to facilitate communications or the development of participatory mechanisms that would stimulate productivity. Any organization that wishes to survive or simply to remain healthy must periodically divest itself of those parts or characteristics that contribute to its malaise (Shafritz et al., p. 275). An organization is not static; it is dynamic. Leaders or administrators should change policy all the time to enhance internally and externally the organization.

Shafritz et al. (2005) argue that OD itself is not a philosophy. It is an approach or strategy for increasing organizational effectiveness. As a process, it has no value biases, but it is usually associated with the idea that effectiveness is found by integrating the individual's associated with the idea that effectiveness is found by integrating the individual's desire for growth with organizational goals. There is no universal OD model that can easily be plugged into a troubled organization. The basic task of the OD adviser is to adapt appropriate portions of the generally available OD technology to the immediate demands of his or her organizational problem (p. 275). OD is not a philosophy. Still, it allows leaders or administrators who are innovators to always ponder about changing policy that might be an advantage for the organization. Due to the 911 attacks, many American intelligence agencies, such as the CIA and FBI, develop new strategies to avoid any internal or external attacks against American interests.

Crosby & Bryson (2005) assert that the development of policymakers' support for a proposal requires cultivating networks. This is especially true in the legislative arena, but also important in the corporate or nonprofit boardroom, the executive cabinet, and administrative offices. The focus here is on the legislative arena because it is crucial in adopting policies that have general application and spur decision making in other arenas (p.293). It is the leader's primary role thinking about development policy in all arenas; his/her role is to think about what section of the organization that needs to change or innovation.

Leaders (Crosby & Bryson, 2005) ensure that the organization develops flexible, transparent, just, and compassionate governance, administrative, and employee – development systems that develop and sustain the organization's core competencies (Light 1998; Collins and Porras, 1997). The organizational systems should also allow conflict to surface so that the organizational is able to learn from varying perspectives, support organizational members' efforts to carry out the mission, and respond to stakeholder needs (p.87). It is the same issue for the church organization. As an organization, it should be flexible and transparent. Most church leaders consider the church administration as a personal business. They do not allow their members to know the church's economic activities. They always ask for money; they still have a project. However, they never present an accurate report of the church activities. They often hire only their family members or close friends in their administration. In the members' meeting, if one asks a question about the accounting system, how it works, they consider him/her as an enemy or someone who should not be the church member. This behavior harms a lot the evangelical system. If God does not attract someone to become a Christian, no one will accept Jesus as his/her savior.

A process framework (Stillman II, 2010) for collaboration suggests that collaboration occurs over time as organizations interact formally and informally through repetitive sequences of negotiation, development of commitments (p.288). The primary key to the success of an organization is commitment. If all organization members commit to seeing developing their organization, they should be positive and have the determination to achieve their goals, whatever the circumstances or any inconvenient they might find.

A. ORGANIZATION THEORY

An organization (Shafritz et al., 2009) is a group of people who jointly work to achieve at least one common goal. A "theory" is a proposition or set of propositions that seek to explain or predict something. The something is the case of organization theory is how groups and individuals behave in differing organizational arrangements. This is critically important information for any manager or leader. It is not an exaggeration to say that the world is ruled by the underlying premises of organization theory. This has been true ever since humankind first organized itself for hunting, war, and even family life. Leaders in every field during every age used organization theory as naturally as they used their oratorical powers (p. 234). The church leaders use organizational theory. A church has different organizations, and each organization has a committee.

VI

The Impact of Personality

HRIS ARGYRIS, A PREEMINENT ANALYST OF ORGANIZATIONAL phenomena for over four decades, first became noteworthy with the publication of his 1957 book *Personality and Organization*. In it he claimed that there was an inherent conflict between the mature adult personality and the needs of modern organizations. The problem, simply put, was that most organizations were treating adults like children. As the truth of this finding was made increasingly evident, ways of treating employees changed. A new dogma evolved that organizations should give their citizens all the responsibilities they could handle—and then some (Shafritz et al., p.279). An organization that wants to be successful should not treat employees like children. The better an organization treats its employees, the better they work to make it successful. If an organization considers its employees like children, they will act like children. They work to make money, but they will not take the job seriously. It is the same approach for a church organization; the pastor should not treat their collaborators as children. We all work for God; we must respect each other. Some pastors don't respect their collaborators. It should not be like that. We all are servants of God; we should respect each other.

The issue here is inherent temperament. According to

journalist Winifred Gallagher, there is still much to be said for the validity of four basic human temperaments first described in ancient Greece by Hippocrates 2,500 years ago. His four "humors" are still commonly used today to informally describe personality types. We have all seen people who are sanguine (optimistic and energetic), melancholic (moody and withdrawn), choleric (irritable and impulsive), and phlegmatic (calm and slow). Indeed, many people have displayed all of these "humors" or moods at one time or another (Shafritz et al. , p.279). One who knows his/her task does not want his/her supervisor to tell him/her what to do. With the job assignments, he/she would know what to do. However, some people have childish behavior by nature, who want to play and do not focus on their activities. If you know they can work as a manager, keep them, but you should always observe what they are doing to persuade them to complete the job assignments. In a local church or a church mission, the leader should apply the right strategy to persuade their members to complete their task without hurting their personality.

The study of organizational behavior Shafritz et al. (2005) includes those aspects of the behavioral sciences that focus on the understanding of human behavior in organizations. There has long considerable interest in the behavior of people inside bureaucracies. After all, the whole purpose of organization theory is to create mechanisms for regulating the behavior of people in organizations (pp. 270, 1). The character of someone determines his/her leadership; the trait is an important tool in organizational behavior. According to journalist Winifred Gallagher, there is still much to be said for the validity of four basic human temperaments first described in ancient Greece by Hippocrates 2,500 years ago. His four "humors" are still commonly used today to informally describe personality types. We have all seen people who are sanguine (optimistic and energetic), melancholic (moody and withdrawn), choleric (irritable and impulsive), and phlegmatic (calm and slow). Indeed, many people have displayed all of these "humors" or moods at one time or another (p.279). I think it is essential to determine that the old bureaucrats' behavior should redefine to serve better the public.

As a result, all leaders are different ways to do things; it depends on their temperaments. For example, President George W. Bush is an optimistic and energetic leader; people can easily read his determination to accomplish what he desires on his face. Moreover, trait theories could be considered as a complementary of organizational behavior. According to Shafritz et al. (2009), the trait approach to leadership assumes that leaders possess traits – personality characteristics – that make them fundamentally different from followers. Advocates of trait theory believe that some people have unique leadership characteristics and qualities that enable them to assume responsibilities not everyone can execute. Therefore, they are born leaders (p. 389). Every leader has his/her way to complete a task, but all will get the same outcome but differently to implement policies. For example, we might face many successful leaders and scholars in public administration conference, but all would not have the same approach. Then we should listen to all of them, and how they become successful. Also, we would not be able to apply the strategy of one of them because we cannot have the same behavior or trait.

Probably the most damaging criticism of trait theory (Shafritz et al., 2009), however, has been its lack of ability to identify which traits make an effective leader. Even among the traits that have been most commonly cited – intelligence, energy, achievement, dependability, and socioeconomic status – there is a lack of consensus across studies. The most obvious proof that leadership involves more than possessing certain traits is the simple fact that a leader may be effective in one setting and ineffective in another. It all depends on the situation (p.390). No one can determine which character is valid or not. That is why we cannot imitate someone successful in his/her organization; all can advance different approaches and have the same outcome, which is a success.

Authoritarian leaders determined all policies, set all work assignments, were personal in their criticisms, and were product (or task) oriented. Democratic leaders shared decision - making powers with subordinates, left decisions about assignments up to the group, and participated in groups activities but tried not to monopolize. Laissez-faire leaders allowed freedom for individual and group decision – making, provided information (or supplies) only when requested, and did not participate in the group except when called upon. They functioned more as facilitators (p.391). All those leaders use the different political systems, but they all have the same outcome. All leaders do not have the same trait, do not use the same political system, and the same philosophy or strategy, but they accomplish their success. It is excellent to listen to all organization's leaders and their strategy, but their philosophy or strategy would not apply to any other organization. What is essential to observe is the discipline, commitment, and determination. Without this trichotomy, no one will be able to be successful. Crosby & Bryson (2005) assert that without the commitment of key implementers, change is likely to wither on the vine. It may be given lip service but displaced by other priorities and needs. Of course, implementers who were part of the advocacy coalition that supported adoption of the change are likely to be supportive. Many, however, will not have participated in the coalition, and policy entrepreneurs and policy makers must give them incentives to allocate time, energy, and other organizational resources to implementation (p.314). Then commitment remains the key to policy implementation. Whatever the system, the trait, the philosophy, or strategy that someone can use, commitment, discipline, and determination are the keys to success.

VII

Cultural Aspects

WHEN SOCIOLOGISTS TALK ABOUT CULTURE, RICHARD Peterson ([1979](#)) observed, they usually mean one of four things: *norms, values, beliefs,* or *expressive symbols.* Roughly, norms are the way people behave in a given society, values are what they hold dear, beliefs are how they think the universe operates, and expressive symbols are representations, often of social norms, values, and beliefs themselves. In the last decades of the twentieth century, sociologists added a fifth item to the list: *practices.* Culture in this recent view describes people's behavior patterns, not necessarily connected to any particular values or beliefs. We discuss these various meanings later, but for now the point is that even such specialists as cultural sociologists use the word *culture* to stand for a whole range of ideas and objects (Griswold, p. 3).

Each ethnic group's culture differs from each other. Leaders should have general knowledge in culture to better know how to deal with each ethnic group. For example, people's same body language in many countries or regions does not have the same meaning. You can make a body language with a positive connotation; the same body language can have a pessimistic sense for someone else. There are church members from all regions in the country; they have their own norms, values, beliefs, and expressive symbols.

A. LIFESTYLE

Hypocrisy, betrayal, egocentrism, jealousy, violence, hatred, superstitious Poverty, crime, teenage pregnancy, high infant mortality rates, racism, urban decay, unemployment, drugs, drunk driving, inadequate health care—and on and on. Most of us can reel off a list of pressing social problems without hesitation. Although such a list has roots in problems that cause human suffering universally—such as violence, hatred, and premature death—the forms that these problems take are specific to each culture and society (Griswold, p. 104). People who are Christians always think that Christians are perfect; we cannot make any mistake. As Christians, we are trying to avoid anything against God's law, but it does not mean we are perfect. We are trying to have a different lifestyle than those who are not Christians. Therefore, if anyone is in Christ, he is a new creation; the old has gone, the new has come (2 Corinthians 5:17). If all people become Christians, the world will be better; we will have a world without crime, violence, hatred, and immorality. However, as human beings, we can also make mistakes like anyone.

B. EDUCATION

The analysis starts with an observation: Everywhere in Europe, Protestants flocked to commerce, business, and skilled labor far more than Catholics; they were, in other words, overrepresented in capitalist economic activities. Weber considered the spirit of capitalism as involving an ethic or duty, particularly one's duty in a calling, as exemplified by such aphorisms of Benjamin Franklin as "Time is money" (Griswold, p. 36).

Some Christians from underdeveloped countries usually think they should not be involved in business activities to serve God better. Others believe they can do business only to survive but not a big one because wealthy people will not heir the heaven. They misunderstand the parable of the rich man and Lazarus. Both died; the angels carried Lazarus to Abraham's side while the rich man was in hell, where he was in torment (Luke 16:22). The rich man goes to hell because he did not correctly administer his wealth; he was very selfish. He did not help poor people. Lazarus, the beggar, was at his gate, but he ignored Lazarus to help him. Christians can be wealthy, but they should help others. As a Christian, it is not fair to have a lot of money and don't help those in need. However, if you are poor, you struggle to change your life while it does not change, but you try. In this case, you do not have to do any bad things to become rich or hate others who are rich. You should praise God and accept your condition. However, if you stay without doing nothing, you are against God's law because He has created us to work.

C. COMMUNITY COLLABORATION

Community collaboration plays a significant role in public administration; citizens' participation in public affairs encourages decision-makers to implement policies that could benefit the entire community. Morse (2010) argues that in most places, leaders and citizens simply do not know how to collaborate. By exploring stories of successful collab- oration, community leaders and citizens can learn to design; initiate and sustain collaborative initiatives to address issues of shared concern in their cities and regions (p. 129). A community cannot make progress if the citizens and the community leaders do not work together; the citizens should know their community's needs and share them with the local leaders.

In 1983 citizens' perceptions that the city, explained Morse, was in the control of a few individuals resulted in a successful campaign to establish a district-based election of city council members in place of an at- large election system. Citizens were moving in the direction of more involvement in city affairs, stronger neighborhoods, and more citizen associations. In 1988 Mayor Goddard invited the people of Phoenix and the surrounding communities to become involved in a long-range planning process to be guided by the new Citizen Policy Committee. The project became known as the Phoenix Futures Forum and was funded by the city and several private organizations. The Forum essentially became a process-one that encouraged participation by all business, labor, religious, nonprofit, neighborhood, environmental, and educational groups, in addition to city officials. Over the two years of the Forum's work, the citywide forums, work sessions, and neighborhood forums became credible outlets for citizen concerns and visions. Somewhere between 1,500 and 3,500 citizens participated in the process (Morse, p.133). The citizens in a community should have their eyes opened on their community to know what is going on, does the administration go well or not? If it does not go well, they have to encourage the local government to make the right decisions to fix the problems.

Official policy-makers have the legal authority to engage in the formation of public policy. (Of course, some who have the legal authority to act may in fact be significantly influenced by others, such as important constituents or pressure groups.) These include legislators, executives, administrators, and judges. Each performs policymaking tasks that are at least somewhat functionally different from those of the others. It is useful to differentiate between primary and supplementary policy-makers. Primary policy-makers have direct constitutional authority to act; for example, Congress does not have to depend upon other government units for authorization to enact legislation. Supplementary policy-makers, such as national administrative agencies, however, operate on the basis of authority granted by others (primary policy-makers). This puts secondary policy-makers in a dependency relationship. Administrative agencies, such as the Federal Trade Commission and the Bureau of Land Management, that derive their operating authority from congressional legislation will typically need to be responsive to congressional interests and requests. Congress may retaliate against unresponsive agencies by imposing restrictions on their authority or reducing their budgets. On the other hand, Congress has little need to be solicitous about agency interests (Anderson, p. 48).

A recent study conducted by Richard Harwood (1991) for the Kettering Foundation tells a very different story. Rather than being apathetic or unconcerned, citizens are angry and frustrated by politics as usual. They feel cut out of the process, unheard and unable to see how they can have any real impact on public affairs. Government is out of the reach of ordinary citizens. It does not respond to the concerns and needs of individuals, neighborhoods, or com- munities but to interest groups and power players. Dennis Burke of the Phoenix Futures Forum (PFF) says, "People don't see any values in their economic or political lives that relate to what they want to have in their personal lives"(Morse, p.95). Then, the citizens' participation in community affairs helps the government to be more active in the development community.

But citizens desperately want to be engaged in public life. They want their views to be heard, understood, and considered. They want to have a sense that their involvement can make a difference that the public, not governments or interest groups, defines the public interest. Burke, a PFF task-force member, describes the purpose of the Forum as a way to 'put government and citizens intimately in touch with each other so that one is the reflection of the other and so the government is a reflection of the kind of community the people want' (Morse, 95, 6). Citizens of a community should engage in public life; they could not neglect their community. They should involve in all community affairs to the benefit of their community.

Morse continues to explain that citizens ask for forums that can provide constructive ways for them to work together with governments on common problems. They would like to have information and problem-solving opportunities that go beyond the polarization of exclusive partisan positions. They want intimate and direct contact with the issues and problems that concern them. Most of all, they want a sense of com- munity-a sense that all of us are in this together. There is no lack of desire in citizens to participate in public affairs. 'I want to participate in my community,' comments a Phoenix citizen. 'I want more say in what goes on.' Fed up with gridlock and impotence, citizens are creating new methods of public involvement. Faced with a paucity of formal options for engaging constructively with governments around issues of shared concern, citizens are turning to themselves for leadership and initiative. They are tackling difficult problems not in anarchic or antagonistic ways but in ways that reflect a new kind of democracy and sense of citizenship. It is a deeper, more intimate, and more inclusive kind of democracy--one that is more direct than representative and more consensual than majoritarian. It is a shift in the practice of democracy from hostility to civility, from advocacy to engagement, from confrontation to conversation, from debate to dialogue, and from separation to community (Morse, p.96). The citizens' involvement in community affairs enhances democracy in the community because they help the government.

Just what is collaboration? That concept, explained Morse, as we use it, goes beyond communication, cooperation, and coordination. As its Latin roots-com and laborare-indicate, it means "to work together." It is a mutually beneficial relationship between two or more parties who work toward common goals by sharing responsibility, authority, and accountability for achieving results. Collaboration is more than simply sharing knowledge and information (communication) and more than a relationship that helps each party achieve its own goals (cooperation and coordination). The purpose of collaboration is to create a shared vision and joint strategies to address concerns that go beyond the purview of any particular party (Morse, p.97). Then the collaboration is vital to develop a community (a church). The citizens should organize themselves in association to determine their community's needs, and they should work together with their local government. Some citizens think that the government is the enemy of them, which is not true; it is not the citizens' enemy, but if they do not let the government know the needs of the community, the government itself has to determine what is good for the community.

Well-structured problems, according to Dunn, are those that involve one or a few decision makers and a small set of policy alternatives. Utilities (values) reflect goal consensus and are clearly ranked in order of decision makers' preferences. The outcomes of each alternative are known either with complete certainty (deterministically) or within acceptable margins of probable error (risk). The prototype of the well-structured problem is the completely computerized decision problem, with which all consequences of all policy alternatives are programmed in advance. Relatively low-level operational problems in public agencies provide illustrations of well-structured problems. For example, problems of replacing agency vehicles are relatively simple ones that involve finding the optimum point at which an old vehicle should be traded for a new one, taking into account average repair costs for older vehicles and purchasing and depreciation costs for new ones (Dunn, p. 73). The council at Jerusalem is a great example of consensus to resolve the conflict between some men came down from Judea to Antioch and want to convince the Christians to circumcise. Paul and Barnabas listened to them carefully and explained them their doctrine is an old-fashioned because the church is not under the law dispensation.

Furthermore, Paul and Barnabas go to encounter all fathers of the apostolic church at Jerusalem to end this dispute.

Some men came down from Judea to Antioch and were teaching the brothers: 'Unless you are circumcised, according to the custom taught by Moses, you cannot be saved.' This brought Paul and Barnabas into sharp dispute and debate with them. So Paul and Barnabas were appointed, along with some other believers, to go up to Jerusalem to see the apostles and elders about this question. The church sent them on their way, and as they traveled through Phoenicia and Samaria, they told how the Gentiles had been converted. This news made all the brothers very glad. When they came to Jerusalem, they were welcomed by the church and the apostles and elders, to whom they reported everything God had done through them. Then some of the believers who belonged to the party of the Pharisees stood up and said, 'The Gentiles must be circumcised and required to obey the law of Moses.' The apostles and elders met to consider this question. After much discussion, Peter got up and addresses them: 'Brothers, you know that some time ago God made a choice among you that the Gentiles might hear from my lips the message of the gospel and believe. God, who knows the heart, showed that he accepted them by giving the Holy Spirit to them, just as he did to us. He made no distinction between us and them, for he purified their hearts by faith. … When they finished, James (the Pastor, the brother of Jesus) spoke up: 'Brothers, listen to me. Simeon has described to us how God at first showed his concern by taking from the Gentiles a people for himself. The words of the prophets are in agreement with this, as it is written: After this I will return and rebuild David's fallen tent. Its ruins I will rebuild, and I will restore it, that the remnant of men may seek the Lord, and all the Gentiles who bear my name, says the Lord, who does these things that have been known for ages. It is my judgment, therefore, that we should not make it difficult for the Gentiles who are turning to God. … Then the apostles and elders, with the whole church, decided to choose some of their own men and send to Antioch with Paul and Barnabas. They chose Judas (called Barsabbas) and Silas, two men who were leaders among the brothers. With them they sent the following letter: The apostles and elders, your brothers, to the Gentile believers in Antioch, Syria and Cilicia: Greetings (Acts 15:1-18). This consensus allowed all Antioch's leaders and Christians to serve their God without any confusion or thinking about the law dispensation.

Rainey asserts that the effects of the political and institutional environment of public organizations on the people in those organizations show up in numerous ways. In recent decades, governments at all levels in the United States and in other nations have mounted efforts to reform civil service systems and government pay systems (In- graham, 1993; Peters and Savoie, 1994; Gore, 1993; Thompson, 2000; U.S. Office of Management and Budget, 2002). Typically, the reformers have sought to correct allegedly weak links between performance and pay, promotion, and discipline, claiming that these weak links undermine motivation and hence performance and efficiency. These reforms have come about not just because of public attitudes but also because government managers have for years complained about having insufficient authority over pay, promotion, and discipline (Macy, 1971; U.S. Office of Personnel Management, 1983, 1999, 2001). The reforms also reflect, then, the constraints on public managers that earlier chapters have described. That such reforms have often foundered or backfired (Ingraham, 1993; Kellough and Lu, 1993; Perry, Petrakis, and Miller, 1989) raises the possibility that these con- straints are inevitable in the public sector (Rainey, Facer, and Bozeman, 1995) (Rainey, p. 221). The church is also an institution like any other institution. It should be reformed over time because it is not static, but it is dynamic. Many reformers, such as Hus, Savonarola, Wiclef, Luther, as many others, fought for a better church. Our generation should continue to fight for it.

Institutionalism assumes the centrality of leadership,

management, and professionalism; it comprehends theory development all the way from the supervision of street-level bureaucrats to the transformational leadership of entire institutions (Smith and Lipsky 1993; Maynard-Moody and Musheno 2003). Institutionalism recognizes the salience of action or choice and defines choice as expressions of expectations of consequences (March and Olsen 1984). In the modern world of productivity, performance, and outcomes measurement, institutionalism reminds us that institutions and those associated with them shape meanings, rely on symbols, and seek an interpretive order that obscures the objectivity of outcomes. Institutionalism is particularly useful in the disarticulated state because its assumptions do not rest primarily on sovereignty and authority; they rest instead on the patterns of politics, order, and shared meaning found in governmental as well as nongovernmental institutions (Frederickson 1999) (Smith, p. 71).

For some, the impulse to engage in public processes extends beyond voting, going to community meetings or public hearings, writing letters or e-mails, or engaging in focus groups and visioning projects. It leads to a full- time commitment to engage in what we typically call "public service." The call to public service that many people experience is based on the responsibility of all citizens to serve, but it goes far beyond this responsibility, to become a full-time occupation, even a preoccupation. The public servant may be someone who runs for and serves in elective public office, perhaps for a short time, perhaps throughout a career; but he or she may also be someone who works in an agency of government—in social services, public health, environmental protection, law enforcement, or any one of myriad other public and governmental agencies. Today the public servant may even be someone who works outside government, perhaps in a nonprofit organization or in a public advocacy role. Wherever public servants are found, they are likely to be motivated by the desire to make a difference, to improve the lives of others, to do something meaningful with their own lives, to do something 'significant' (Denhardt, p.55). A church member has the same role as a public servant. He/she should do everything allowing the church to progress spiritually, economically, and socially. The church should contribute to the development of the community. The church's leaders must have a significant relationship with the local government. A church is a protection for society; it contributes to decreasing the rate of crime and immorality.

VIII

Church organization

THE WORD CHURCH IS MENTIONED FOR THE FIRST TIME BY Jesus in Matthew 16: 18 'And I tell you that you are Peter, and on this rock I will build my church, and the gates of Hades will not overcome it'. The church is an institution built by Jesus Christ; He is the founder of His church. It could be persecuted but not destroyed because it is not an organization made by a human being. Since its foundation after the Holy Spirit Comes at Pentecost, it has known many periods of persecution; even it becomes weak or polluted, but the church is still existing and waiting for His Master. Jesus has trained His disciples to be ready to work in this organization, and after the Pentecost, His disciples applied His methods allowing the church to grow up. The book of Acts is a history book of the apostolic church, the first one, which is the sample that all churches should follow to enhance the church of Christ.

A. HIERARCHY

Jesus-Christ builds the evangelical church; He is the Chief Executive Officer (CEO) of the Church; He is the Chief cornerstone. Apostle

Peter asserts that to you who believe, He is precious; but to those who are disobedient, 'The stone which the builders rejected has become the chief cornerstone', and 'A stone of stumbling and a rock of offense' (I Peter 2: 7, 8). He is an organizational, a visionary, and a charismatic leader.

One cannot be a leader without followers; Jesus, as a leader, had built a network system with twelve people that he was considered as his disciples or students. They had different characteristics, but He trained them to know how to deal with each other and accept each other's view point. The Zebedee's sons ambition express clearly the leadership of Jesus; the mother of Zebedee's sons came to Him with her sons, kneeling down and asking something from Him. And He said to her, "What do you wish?" She said to Him, "Grant that these two sons of mine mat sit, one on Your right hand and the other on the left, in your kingdom." But Jesus answered and said, "You do not know what you ask. Are you able to drink the cup that I am about to drink, and be baptized with the baptism that I am baptized with?" They said to Him, 'We are able.'...And when the ten heard it, they were greatly displeased with the two brothers. But Jesus called them to Himself and said, "You know that the rulers of the Gentiles lord it over them, and those who are great exercise authority over them. Yet it shall not be so among you; but whoever desires to become great among you, let him be your servant. And whoever desires to be first among you, let him be your slave – just as the Son of Man did not come to be served, but to serve, and to give His life a ransom for many" (Matthew 20:20-28). Jesus, as a great leader, has controlled the anger of those ten disciples who felt very mad against the ambition of Zebedee's sons.

It is not without reason He taught those twelve young men; as a visionary leader, He knew that His ministry on earth was limited; His mission on earth is almost over. Then He has to teach His philosophy to others to expand His philosophy or His doctrine. A visionary leader should think about making disciples to continue his/her philosophy. Apostle Paul teaches Timothy and says, 'the things that you have heard from me among many witnesses, commit these to faithful men who will be able to teach others also' (II Timothy 2: 2). A leader who does not make disciples is not a leader; his/her ministry is over when he/she passes away. His/her name goes in the grave forever, but someone who makes disciples cannot die even his/her body is in the grave. For example, Socrates, the modern philosophy father, did not write any book, but he made disciples. We, as scholars, know Socrates by Plato his disciple and Aristotle the disciple of Plato.

As a great teacher, Jesus, most of the time, taught his disciples by questioning them; that technique was used before by Socrates. Then the Socratic' methods could be considered also as Jesus' method. I think His first question to the disciples is 'You are the salt of the earth; but if the salt loses its flavor, how shall it be seasoned? He did not let the disciples answered that question. He gave them the answer. He asked them that question to get their attention. He has continued to use the Socratic method in the Beatitudes. He says, ' You have heard that it was said, 'You shall love your neighbor and hate your enemy.' 'But I say to you 'love your enemies, bless those who curse you, do good to those who hate you, and pray for those who spitefully use you and persecute you', … For if you love those who love you, what reward have you? Do not even the tax collectors do the same? And if you greet your brethren only, what do you do more than others? Do not even the tax collectors do so? (Matthew 5: 43-47). An important question that Jesus wanted an answer from His disciples is about who is he to make sure the disciples know precisely who he is? What is His mission? When Jesus came into the region of Caesarea Philippi, He asked His disciples, saying, Who do men say that I, the Son of Man, am? So they said, Some say John the Baptist, some Elijah, and others Jeremiah or one of the prophets. He said to them, but who do you say that I am? Simon Peter answered and said, You are the Christ, the Son of the living God. Jesus answered and said to him, blessed are you, Simon Bar-Jonah, for flesh and blood has not revealed this to you, but My Father who is in heaven. And I also say to you that you are Peter, and on this rock I will build my church, and the gates of Hades shall not prevail against it (Matthew 16: 13-18). I focus on the conversation of Jesus about who he is to His disciples to make sure all my readers know that Jesus is the CEO, the Chief of the church. As Church leaders, we have to understand that the church does not belong to us but to Jesus. It does not mean that you have to let people do whatever they want as a shepherd; if you do so, He has to question you about the ministry that He has given you. God has to punish the false shepherds; He told Ezekiel to say that to the shepherds of Israel: 'You eat the fat and clothe yourselves with the wool; you slaughter the fatlings, but you do not feed the flock. The weak you have not strengthened, nor have you healed those who were sick, nor bound up the broken, nor brought back what was driven away, nor sought what was lost; but with force and cruelty you have ruled them. So they were scattered because there was no shepherd; and they became food for all the beasts of the field when they were scattered. My sheep wandered through all the mountains, and on every high hill; yes, My flock was scattered over the whole face of the earth, and no one was seeking or searching for them... '(Ezekiel 34: 2-10). A Pastor, as a leader, a follower of Jesus-Christ, has to follow the path of his/her master not as the CEO of the church but as general manager.

It is not without reason Jesus after his resurrection before his ascension talks specially to Peter to teach him a final lesson to make sure he knows how to take care of His lambs. ' So when they had eaten breakfast, Jesus said to Simon Peter, ' Simon, son of Jonah, do you love Me more than these? He said to Him, 'Yes, Lord; You know that I love you.' He said to him, ' Feed My lambs. He said to him again a second time, ' Simon, son of Jonah, do you love Me? He said to Him, Yes, Lord; you know that I love you.' He said to him, Tend My sheep,' He said to him the third time, ' Simon, son of Jonah, do you love Me?' And he said to Him, 'Lord,

You know all things; You know that I love you,' Jesus said to him, Feed My sheep' (John 21: 13-17). Jesus gave Peter a final exam to make he is qualified for the job.

And ten days after the ascension of Jesus (40 days after his resurrection plus ten days after his ascension= Pentecostal), Peter had proved the Master that he is qualified for the Job. they were all filled with the Holy Spirit and began to speak with other tongues, as the Spirit gave them utterance (Acts 2: 4) ... So they were all amazed and perplexed, saying to one another,' Whatever could this mean?' Others mocking said, 'They are full of new wine' (v. 12, 13). But Peter, standing up with the eleven, raised his voice and said to them, 'Men of Judea and all who dwell in Jerusalem, let this be known to you, and heed my words (v.14). Peter tells them about the prophecy of Pentecost and Jesus-Christ they just crucified. He was not the same Peter when Jesus was in the hands of evil people. When one fills with the Spirit, he/she cannot be afraid, to tell the truth to sinful people. Peter was so active to expand the doctrine of Jesus-Christ; he preached the gospel under the control of the Holy Spirit, and all disciples did the same.

Consequently, Peter and other disciples proved clearly that their Master did a great job as a visionary and organizational leader. The church of Christ remains a strong organization because the Master made disciples; if He did not make disciples, the church would not be healthy. An organization cannot be vital if the CEO of that organization does not make disciples. The church's pastor becomes just after Jesus; if Jesus comes after him, the church does not belong to Christ. Then that church could not be the church of Christ. All disciples followed the Master; the leaders of the primitive church had respect for each other; they knew how to deal with each other because they had followed the path of their Master, who taught them humility. They knew their function. For example, there was an administrative problem at the beginning of the church; Hebrews widows had more considerations than Hellenists widows. There arose a complaint against the Hebrews by the Hellenists because their widows were neglected in the daily distribution. Then the twelve summoned the multitude of the disciples and said we shouldn't leave God's word and serve tables. Therefore, brethren, seek out from among you seven men of good reputation, full of the Holy Spirit and wisdom, whom we may appoint over this business. Still, we will give ourselves continually to prayer and the ministry of the word (Acts 6: 1-4). The disciples could not involve in all activities, and they appointed seven great leaders to manage the daily distribution activities.

A Pastor, as general manager, should not involve in all activities in the church organization; he /she should appoint people that have excellent credit to manage some activities. Jethro, Moses' father-in-law, explained to Moses why he could not deem the people by himself; he says that both you and these people who are with you will surely wear yourselves out. For this thing is too much for you; you are not able to perform it by yourself (Exodus 18: 18). Also, a Pastor who does not share the tasks, his/her followers would not respect him/her because a great leader should not appear all the time in front of his/her followers. If he/she does so, his/her people would consider him/her as an ordinary person and treat him/her as a familiar person.

In Revelation, Jesus is written the letters to the seven churches of Asia; He addressed every single letter to the angel of the church, which is a symbol of respect for the leader of the local church. Bruce (1986) asserts that the messages to the churches follow an easily recognized pattern. The risen Christ, designating Himself by one of His titles, addresses the 'angel' of the church with the words 'I know'; there follows a brief description of the condition of the church with appropriate commendation or reproof, promise or warming (p.1601). Jesus addressed the letter to the local pastor because he respects his accountability as the general manager of the church; second, the Pastor (angel) is the first one after Jesus who knows the church's situation if it wealthy spiritually or not. Then the recommendation to Jesus is fair, and the local Pastor cannot complaint against His recommendation because he knows very well as the shepherd the situation of the church. No one can see the condition of the local church than the leader who leads the church. Then it is not without reason Jesus addressed His letter to each Pastor individually of the seven churches.

Even though Jesus' brothers were not among the disciples while Jesus was on earth, but after His resurrection, they believed in His power. Then they were among the disciples in the upper room to wait for the Holy Spirit. '... These all continued with one accord in prayer and supplication, with the women and Mary the mother of Jesus, and with His brothers' (Acts 1:14). James, one of the brothers of Jesus, became the Pastor of the Jerusalem church, and all first disciples of Christ paid attention to him as the leader. They did not say he was not with Jesus in His ministry, but He led the church; they respected him as a leader without thinking that a is a newcomer in Jesus' ministry.

Herod killed James, John's brother; just after this horrible action, he thought about killing also Peter. But God sent an angel to deliver him from the prison. Peter went to prayer house and knocked at the door; when they opened it, "... motioning to them with his hand to keep silent, he declared to them how the Lord had brought him out of prison. And he said, 'Go, tell these things to James and the brethren" (Acts 12: 17).

Why Peter told them to tell his story to James? It is simple; because he was the pastor of the church. At the church's genesis, some Judaism Christians wanted to persuade the gentiles believers to circumcise; Paul and Barnabas went to Jerusalem to encounter James the pastor of Jerusalem church and elders, to discuss this issue. Paul, a great intellectual, had a lot of knowledge, didn't say I do not need any other viewpoint about this issue, but he got respect for the elders; he listened to their viewpoint on that issue. 'Then all the multitude kept silent and listened to Barnabas and Paul declaring how many miracles and wonders God had worked through them among the Gentiles. And after they had become silent, James answered, saying, 'Men and brethren, listen to me:

Simon has declared how God at the first visited the Gentiles to take out of them a people for His name. And with this the words of the prophets agree, just as it is written: ' after this I will return and will rebuild the tabernacle of David, which has fallen down; I will rebuild its ruins, and I will set it up; so that the rest of mankind may seek the Lord, even all the Gentiles who are called by My name, Says the Lord who does all these things.' Known to God from eternity are all His works. Therefore I judge that we should not trouble those from among the Gentiles who are turning to God, but that we write to them to abstain from things polluted by idols, from sexual immorality, from things strangled, and from blood" (Acts 15: 13-20). The important part I would like you to focus on is Paul and Barnabas; they went to Jerusalem to hear a final decision about circumcision.

Consequently, it should be the same for our Christian leaders today; we have to respect the local church's hierarchy. The senior Pastor has the final words in everything. It does not mean he/she is a dictator, but this is how it works. It does not mean also he/she does not need collaborators; he/she needs them for advice, but he/she has the final decision. He/she is like a judge; in some cases, the judge does not have to pronounce a verdict, but the jury members have to decide; however, the final judgment should read by the judge, not a member of the jury. So the Pastor even he/she works in collaboration with others, has to read the final decision. He/she can appoint an assistant Pastor to read a final decision, but an assistant Pastor cannot take any decision for the church without contacting the senior Pastor.

There was no significant conflict among the primitive Christian leaders because they had the same interest, which was preaching and making disciples for Christ, but today some so-called Christian leaders fight for their interest, which is making money not the interest of God. Apostle Paul gave us a great example; there was a controversy in the Corinthian church among those church members. Some members were for Paul, and others are for Apollos. If Paul and Apollos fought for their own interest, the church would be divided, but they worked for God's wisdom. Paul says to them: " Now I plead with you, brethren, by the name of our Lord Jesus Christ, that you all speak the same thing, and that there be no divisions among you, but that you be perfectly joined together in the same mind and in the same judgment. ... Now I say this, that each of you says, I am of Paul, or I am of Apollos, or I am of Cephas, or I am of Christ. Is Christ divided? Was Paul crucified for you? Or were you baptized in the name of Paul (I Corinthians 1: 10-13)?

In chapter three, Paul declares that they are God's fellow workers. 'Who the is Paul, and who is Apollos, but ministers through whom you believed, as the Lord gave to each one? I planted, Apollos watered, but God gave the increase. So then neither he who plants is anything, nor he who waters, but God who gives the boost (I Corinthians 3: 5-7). Today, the church leaders are so different from the first church leaders; today, most church leaders glorify themselves talking all the time about their degree, their church building, even their money, but they do not glorify God. It is excellent to get a degree; I believe in knowledge, and I fight to obtain many doctoral degrees. But we do not have to talk about it again and again. It is excellent to get a church building or a Cathedral, but you do not have to glorify yourself for that. You get a lot of money; it is great, but you do not have to promote yourself for that. All glories are for God. Our God is omniscient, so we should have the knowledge and fight to get more understanding every day. Our God is wealthy; He has created everything, so we should be wealthy, but we should not glorify ourselves because we are wealthy.

1. Pastor & his function

The Pastor comes after Jesus-Christ; he is the chief executive officer (CEO), and he is the President of the church committee, but he can nominate a trustful member to be the President (if he wants to) or a vice-President to assist him. However, the pastor may have his own strategy to create the church committee. His function is to supervise or control all church activities and teach the words of God to the people. Ref. Acts 6: 1-2, Acts 12: 1-19; (v.17) (… go shew these things unto James, and to the brethren); Acts 15: 1-27 (v.2) They determined that Paul and Barnabas, and certain other of them, should go up to Jerusalem unto the apostles and elders about this question; (v.13) James answered….) I Tim. 3, Tite 2.

All the letters to the seven churches in Revelation addressed to the angel of the church (the Pastor) (Rev. 2 & 3). Bruce asserts that "the letters to the churches follow an easily recognized pattern. The risen Christ, designating Himself by one of His titles, addresses the 'angel' of the church with the words 'I know'; there follows a brief description of the condition of the church with appropriate commendation or reproof, promise or warning" (p.1601). Any wrong thing that has occurred in the church, God, the Chief of chiefs, has to address His complaint to the Pastor.

2. Co-Pastor (s) & his or their function

The function of a co-Pastor is to collaborate with the Pastor in chief and assist him in all tasks that he wants to. He/she is also his/her adviser. He/she cannot take any decision without the adhesion of the senior Pastor.

3. Committee and its function

A committee is a group of servants of God that the Pastor nominates, or the church members elect to collaborate with the Pastor for the church's benefit. The committee members' role is not to work against the Pastor but to work with the Pastor.

Furthermore, as a servant of God, the Pastor should avoid fanatics; Paul as a servant of God remains a great example. Marsh, in his commentary, asserts that " Is Christ divided (I Cor.1:13): or,'Is Christ parceled out among you?': Wescott and Hort, with Lightfoot, make the phrase affirmative, but this breaks up the homogeneity of the three-fold interrogative. Paul reduces the situations to basic principles; other leaders cannot take the place of Christ (p.1351)… I planted the seed, Apollos watered it, but God made it grow: … have one purpose: Literally, are one thing (neuter), 'on the same level' (Moffatt); this gives the lie to any accusation of opposing factions that Paul and Apollos were at variance. It is well expressed by NEB, 'they work as a team" (p.1354).

4. Deacons and their function

Readings
Acts 6: 1-8; I Timothy 3

Trenchard argues that, referring to Acts 6:1-8, the language difficulty – some of the disciples were Aramaic-speaking and some Greek-speaking- must have caused real difficulties of administration and the needs of the Hellenistic widows had been overlooked. Up to that time the Twelve had received all the voluntary offerings and had been responsible for their distribution among thousands of believers. The complaint showed that a devolution of ministries was necessary. It was not right that the specific ministry of the Twelve should be subordinated to administrative work (2, 4) and so help was needed. But administration was a delicate matter affecting the well-being of the whole church, so that this humble service required a good reputation, wisdom, and, above all, a manifestation of spiritual power (3). The brethren who helped in the selection of suitable men (3, 5) would naturally bear these conditions in mind, and also, very wisely, thought of presenting

Hellenistic helpers, as is shown by the names of the Seven. There could thus be no further thought of favouritism in favour of the Aramaic-speaking community (p.1279).

The deacon (I Tim.3: 8-13) Commentary of Alan G. Nute

The word diakonos, found some thirty times in the NT, is customarily translated either servant or minister, and denotes one engaged in rendering some particular service. It is used to describe domestic servants, civil rulers, preachers and teachers, and in a general way to denote Christians engaged in work for their Lord or for each other. This has led many to the conclusion that Paul is not alluding to a specific group within the church, but to all who are active in Christian service of one form or another. On the other hand, the fact that the paragraph follows immediately the one relating to oversees certainly implies that the cases are parallel and these deacons have recognized functions. Support for this view might also be adducted from Phil. 1:1 where Paul sends greetings to 'all the saints in Christ Jesus at Philippi, with the oversees and deacons' (p.147 Some churches do not use the theme 'deacon'. It is not because they ignore it, but they prefer to talk about committee members or elders. It does not matter; all play the same function. However, the institution of deacons has been created due to a controversy at the church's beginning. The Hellenists' widows were neglected in the daily distribution while the Hebrews were not neglected. As a result, the disciples decided to create that institution. We should understand the context of a biblical text to determine how we can use it in our time; we cannot interpret the bible texts literally, but we should place it in the historical context or cultural context. We sometimes give significant consideration to some writings, even make them a doctrine that we should not give tremendous respect. It does not mean we cannot use them to teach a lesson to our generation, but we should think about the reason the writer mentions something.

5. Groups Leaders and their function

All Christians have an identical mission working for the Kingdom of Christ; then, we all should collaborate as members of a local church for its spiritual and social development. In I Corinthians 12:4, Paul argues that there are diversities of gifts, but the same Spirit. So whatever we can do, we should do it not for the Pastor but Christ, the Supreme Chief of the church. "Whatsoever thy hand findeth to do, do it with thy might; for there is no work, nor device, nor knowledge, nor wisdom, in the grave, whither thou goest" (Eccl. 9:10). However, groups' leaders cannot take any decision without negotiating with the Pastor.

6. Decision –making or decision-makers

All leaders might be considered as decision-makers, but they cannot implement any decision without sharing or submitting it to the Pastor in Chief or CEO of the church. All leaders should follow the direction of the Pastor in chief and help him to encourage members to follow his path. Even though he takes a decision that you do not like as members of the committee, you have to talk to him about what should be changed without creating any panic situation or sharing anything to the members or believers.

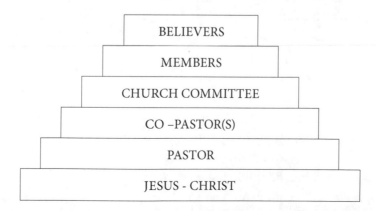

BELIEVERS

MEMBERS

CHURCH COMMITTEE

CO –PASTOR(S)

PASTOR

JESUS - CHRIST

IX

Sunday School

SUNDAY SCHOOL IS AND REMAINS THE ESSENTIAL CHURCH'S entity; it allows it to organize and function very well. It also helps a church to grow in a short period and a tool to help people quickly learn the bible. A knowledgeable pastor was a great student at Sunday school. Even though, at the genesis of this institution, Sunday school's purpose didn't aim only the learning of the bible but helped the abandoned England kids' who worked daily without the attention of anyone. At the same time, "the whole nation, with some few bright exceptions/says Casselts Illustrated History of England, lay in the most deplorable condition of moral and religious destitution possible. The government had ceased to interest itself in almost everything except foreign wars and official corruption; the people at large were left totally without education or moral training..." (archive.org).

I want to elaborate a little about the leadership of Robert Raikes. As a Christian citizen of England, he has observed society's problem and thought about how he could contribute to resolving it. A great citizen of a country should scrutinize what is wrong in his/her community and how one can help to make it better. The following statements explain the problem of England in the eighteenth century: 'It was at this era of darkness, depravity, ignorance, and crime, that John and Charles Wesley and George Whitefield, came forward to preach a revival, and laid the foundation of Methodism one of the most extraordinary instruments of religious, moral, and social regeneration which has appeared in any age of the world, and which not only stands as the far greatest fact of this particular period, but has operated in the great mass of the people an unparalleled life and elevation of mind and character, such as it is difficult to comprehend or calculate, and of which there are few who are fully aware... To alter this disgraceful state of things the Sunday School was founded, and truly amazing was the good result almost immediately produced.' Then Robert Raikes was a transformational leader. He was a citizen who did not cross his arms and complaint about the degradation of his society, but he did something that transforms in a short time his community and continues to change not only England but the entire Christian world.

The Sunday School Society wrote to the latter, stating, that, long before the establishment of the Sunday Schools he had designed a system of universal education, but had met with little support from the clergy and laity, who were alarmed by the magnitude of the undertaking/ He had also vainly attempted to bring of both Houses of parliament. Impressed with Raikes's plan and considering it more practicable than his own, he enlisted the sympathies of Jonas Hanway, the famous traveller, philanthropist, and Russian merchant, whose published travels in Russia and Persia were much read. Hanway was made a commissioner of the Navy, and the Marine Society and the Magdalen Charity owe their establishment mainly to him. He was also, after Raikes and Fox, one of the great promoters of Sundays Schools. In 1786 he wrote Q, comprehensive view of Sunday Schools.

Some people have considered those kids as slaved, and they call them 'white slaves of England'. "One evening he (Raikes) walked down St. Catherine's Street to look for his gardener. Suddenly, he saw a group of ragged children. They looked just as poor and overworked as the prisoners he visited. A little boy in a tattered blue shirt swore as he tackled another boy half his size. 'Git your hands offa me!' The little boy yelled as the two of them wrestled on the cobblestones. Soon a crowd of children gathered around, noisily cheering. 'Hey, stop fighting!' Robert shouted at them as he pulled the two boys apart. 'Go home, all of you'. As the children walked away, Robert asked the gardener's wife, 'who are these children?' 'Ah, pay no mind to them,' she answered. 'Everyone calls them the white slaves of England.' 'Slaves?' asked Robert. 'They work 12 hours a day or longer in the mills and sweatshops', the woman answered. 'Most of their parents are in prison or dead.' Robert cringed. He knew that if his father had died when he was little, he could have been one of these poor children. 'When do they go to school?' he asked. And Sundays are the worst. It's their only day off and they run around like wild animals!' Sunday Schools started. Robert knew that the future was grim for these children who had to work all the time with no hope of an education. Worse yet, with no one to teach them the good news of the Gospel or how to live God's way, they were likely to end up cold, sick and starving in the dreadful prisons. An idea began to form in Robert's mind which he shared with his friend, Reverend Thomas Stock. 'Let's start a Sunday school!' said Robert, 'School on Sunday?' asked Thomas. 'Yes, school on Sunday!' answered Robert. 'We'll teach them to read and write part of the day and teach them the Bible for the rest of the day.' 'It's a great idea!' said Thomas" (www.christianity.com).

Sunday school has been founded to help abandoned kids' workers, but it is not only served to transform them but it serves also to transform adults' life. Burton, E.D. and Mathews, S. argue that the Sunday school is somewhat more than a school, if by a school is meant simply a place for learning and reciting lessons. Some of its exercises belong rather to worship than instruction. Its characterization as the children's church, most unfortunate in some respects, is not wholly wrong. But instruction holds, or certainly ought to hold, the central place. The Sunday school is essentially a school, an educational institution, of the bible (p.3). Then Sunday school is and remains an important tool to transform the lives of those who accept to be a member of it. Unfortunately, in some societies like Haitian Christian churches, people do not get too much interest in Sunday school. The church remains almost empty during the Sunday school, but all members are present at the service. I think it is like that in many Christian churches.

The American Christian leaders have used Sunday school institution not only for the growing of the church but to educate better children and adults in God's way for a better society. Boylan A.M. asserts that the founding of Sunday schools began in urban areas in the 1790s as an attempt to provide rudimentary instruction in reading, writing and religion to working children who, in the view of founders like Benjamin Rush and Samuel Slater, lacked other means of acquiring this knowledge. These schools quickly died out, to be replaced in the 1810s by new Sunday schools evolved from these later schools which by 1832 numbered over 8000, and enrolled almost ten percent of American children aged 5 to 14 (p.36).

Dwight Lyman Moody, one of the great American Evangelist/ Pastor, was not only a Sunday school student, but he has used Sunday school as a tool to transform Chicago society. His desire was to reach the "lost" youth of the city, the children with little to no education, less than ideal family situations, and poor economic circumstances. Soon the Sunday school outgrew the converted saloon used as a meeting hall. As the classes grew, associates encouraged Moody to begin his own church. Eventually, on Feb.28, 1864, the Illinois Street Church (now The Moody Church) opened in its own building with Moody as Pastor (www.moody.edu).

Moody, as a visionary leader, knew what is wrong in his society, and as did the Sunday school founder, Robert, he campaigned to save the "lost" kids in Chicago Street. That is the job of a real

Christian saving or changing others' lives because Jesus saves us to save others. That the reason Apostle Paul said to Timothy, "And the things you have heard me say in the presence of many witnesses entrust to reliable men who will also be qualified to teach others" (2 Timothy 2:2). A great leader does not only appreciate what other leaders did but also tries to apply what he/she learns or understands from them and use their experience on different occasions to benefit the society.

A. GENERAL COMMITTEE

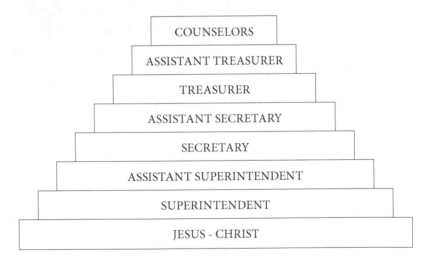

COUNSELORS

ASSISTANT TREASURER

TREASURER

ASSISTANT SECRETARY

SECRETARY

ASSISTANT SUPERINTENDENT

SUPERINTENDENT

JESUS - CHRIST

B. SUNDAY SCHOOL CLASS COMMITTEE

DEVOTION & PRAYER COMMITTEE

VISITING COMMITTEE

TREASURER

ASSISTANT SECRETARY

SECRETARY

ADJUNCT TEACHER

TEACHER (MONITOR)

JESUS - CHRIST

X

Groups Committee

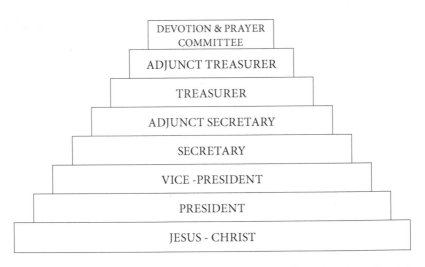

The church's groups are the backbone of the church. They should be well-organized. Each group functions as a little church, but it should follow its rules and doctrine. It contributes to keep the church wealthy spiritually, socially, and financially. It should collaborate with the general committee or the administration of the church. One thing you should have in mind, no one is above the pastor. All committee members are pastor's collaborators. Each member of a committee must know his/ her task and do it well.

XI

Christians' Churches vis-à-vis the Terrorist attacks

SINCE SEPTEMBER 11, 2001, THE WORLD IS COMPLETELY changing. All countries' leaders have focused on the security of their soil to prevent any terrorist attacks. The United States has developed a new political strategy to defend its territories and allies. The administration of President George W. Bush has deemed sine qua non to create another cabinet, which is the Department of Homeland Security.

In private or public administration, leaders should have a vision; that is what they call visionary leadership. If a catastrophe or disaster occurs once, you should think and prepare how to avoid another one; if not, the organization or State would fail.

Eleven days after September 11, 2001, terrorist attacks, Pennsylvania Governor Tom Ridge was appointed as the first Director of the Office of Homeland Security in the White House. The office oversaw and coordinated a comprehensive national strategy to safeguard the country against terrorism and respond to any future attacks. With the passage of the Homeland Security Act by Congress in November 2002, the Department of Homeland Security formally came into being as a stand-alone, Cabinet-level department to further coordinate and unify national homeland security efforts, opening doors on March 1, 2003. Secretary Michael Chertoff took office on February 15, 2005, and initiated a Second Stage Review (2SR) to evaluate the department's operations, policies, and structures. More than 250 members of the department and 18 action teams participate in this effort. The teams also consulted public and private partners at the federal, State, local, tribal, and international levels. On July 13, 2005, Secretary Chertoff announced a six-point agenda, based upon the findings, which included a significant reorganization of the department (www.dhs.gov/creation-department-homeland-security).

Since after 9/11, there are many attacks on Christian Churches (Protestants and Catholics). What should the Christian leaders do to avoid any eventual attacks and protect themselves and their members? Do they take any lesson about what already happened to many churches? First of all, let me enumerate how many attacks against churches, especially African-American Churches, since after 9/11. According to Wikipedia (we can trust that information because we all knew and heard about them), July 11, 2006: A cross was burned outside a predominantly black church in Richmond, Virginia; November 5, 2008: Macedonia Church of God in Christ, in Springfield, Massachusetts, was burned out and an arrest was made; December 28, 2010: In Crane, Texas, the Faith in Christ Church was vandalized with "racist and threatening graffiti" and then firebombed by a man who was attempting to gain entry into the Aryan Brotherhood of Texas; an arrest was made and the perpetrator was found guilty and sentenced to 37 years in prison; November 24, 2014: Flood Christian Church in Ferguson, Missouri, was burned by arsonists during a series of protests over the police shooting of Michael Brown, Jr. Flood Christian is where Michael Brown Sr. was baptized. Some attributed the attack to the protests which burned several other buildings that night, while others said that the building was far from where took place and was more likely burned in retaliation for the comments its pastor had made regarding the release of the officer who had shot Michael Brown, Jr. June 17, 2015: At Emmanuel African Methodist Episcopal Church in Charleston, South Carolina, nine African Americans were shot and killed and a tenth was shot and survived in a mass attack by a white assailant. An arrest was made; June 22, 2015: At College Hill Seventh Day Adventist, in Knoxville, Tennessee, a small fire was set, resulting in minimal damage to the church structure and destruction of the church van. The act was not classified as a hate crime; June 23, 2015: God's Power Church of Christ in Mason, Georgia, was gutted by a fire which was ruled arson; June 24, 2015: At Briar Creek Baptist Church in Charlotte, North Carolina, an unknown arsonist started a three-alarm fire, causing more than $250,000 in damages; November 1, 2016: The-111-year-old Hopewell Missionary Baptist Church in Grenville, Mississippi, was burned and vandalized with the words "Vote Trump" spray-painted onto the building. Officials said during a press conference held on Wednesday, November 2, that the incident was being investigated as a hate crime and Greenville Police Chief Freddie Cannon called the incident "a form of voting intimidation". The arsonist has been identified as a black man who is a member of the church (https://en.wikipedia. org/wiki/list-of-attacks-against-African-American-churches).

What should the Christian leaders do to avoid any eventual attacks and protect themselves and their members? If you know a problem, you can resolve it. Churches' leaders know they have different enemies, then they should not only pray for their protection, but they should make arrangements to get security. During the time of services, they should have volunteers to patrol inside and outside the churches; they can hire two or three security guards with weapons or more if the church is big; they should also have a surveillance camera system.

The Bible does not teach us to cross our hands when the enemies attack us; the Bible gives us many examples. When Nehemiah and his Jews brothers' struggled to build Jerusalem's walls, they had many enemies who wanted to stop them building the walls. Still, Nehemiah prayed God first, and second, he gave some instructions to his brothers to know how they should face their enemies if they attack them. "...Therefore I stationed some of the people behind the lowest points of the wall at the exposed places, posting them by families, with their swords, spears, and bows. After I looked things over, I stood up and said to the nobles, the officials and the rest of the people, 'Don't be afraid of them. Remember the Lord, who is great and awesome, and fight for your brothers, your sons and daughters, your wives, and your homes' (Nehemiah 4: 13-14).

When Judas, the traitor, guided soldiers, and some officials from the chief priests and Pharisees to arrest Jesus, Simon Peter did not cross his hands. He drew his sword and struck the high priest's servant, cutting off his right ear (the servant's name was Malchus). Jesus commanded Peter, 'Put your sword away! Shall I not drink the cup the Father has given me (John 18:10-11)?' If Jesus' ministry were not over on earth, His disciples would not only cut off Malchus' ear, but they would fight and kill a lot of soldiers. Consequently, we do not have to cross our hands and let the enemies kill us, our families, and our brothers and sisters in Christ.

All gun attacks in the United States are not terrorist attacks or hates issues; some are social revenge. One who has conflict in his/her household, workplace, or church may choose to hurt his/her family, coworkers, or his/her brothers and sisters in Christ. Last week, I talked to a friend of mine, about that issue; he argues that most of the time, one who chooses to kill many people in a public place can be sick mentally. He is right! We talked about the gunman in Texas that killed more than two dozen people at the First Baptist Church of Sutherland Springs on November 6, 2017. According to local officials, the shooting did not appear to the fueled or religious issues, as has been the case involving other rampages at houses of worship. Instead, they said the gunman had sent 'threatening texts' to his mother-in-law as part of this ongoing dispute (The Washington Post).

When a gun attack occurs in the United States, some political leaders, social activists, and journalists have questioned the Second Amendment. It protects the citizen's right to keep and bear arms (A well-regulated militia, being necessary to the security of a free State, the right of the people to keep and bear arms, shall not be infringed). I think the problem is not the amendment because everyone should have the right to protect himself, but the way the government deals with those who bear arms. The following questions are: Does the government test the brain of one who has a license to bear arms before he/she gets access to buy weapons? Does the government limit the number and kind of weapon one should have? Does the government control the activities of one who bear arms?

If the government should answer the questions above, they could also resolve the mass shooting problem in the United States. Before one should bear arms, he/she should be evaluated by a medical doctor and psychologist to determine if that person is healthy mentally. Even though someone is healthy mentally, he/she should not have three or more rifles on his/her possession; if someone tries to possess more than one rifle, they should question and observe him/her. The secret service should always have eyes open on those who bear arms, whoever they are. If the government applies the methods above, mass shootings should resolve at 90%.

Every problem has a solution; there is no problem without a solution because God has created us in his image, i.e., with His intelligence or knowledge. All questions have their answers, but we should carefully study the problems until we find the answers. Consequently, attacking Christian churches and mass shootings could resolve if they implement my proposal solution above.

XII

Conclusion

A CHURCH LEADER WHO READS THIS BOOK THOROUGHLY CAN determine different different leadership leadership and know-how to apply them to enhance the church. I encourage all church leaders to teach leadership to the members that can allow them to know their function and contribute to developing the church-organization spiritually and socially. I want to give you the same advice that the apostle Paul gave to Timothy: 'The things you have heard me say in the presence of many witnesses entrust to reliable men who will also be qualified to teach others.' I also want to give you the advice that Jethro gave to Moses: 'The work is too heavy for you; you cannot handle it alone. Listen now to me, and I will provide you some advice, and may God be with you. You must be the people's representative before God and bring their disputes to him. Teach them the decrees and laws and show them how to live and the duties they are to perform. But select capable men from all the people, men who fear God, trustworthy men who hate dishonest gain, and appoint them as officials over thousands, hundreds, fifties and tens. Have them serve as judges for the people at all times but have them bring every difficult case to you; the simple cases they can decide themselves (Exodus 18: 18-22). You do not have to be only a Christian leader to follow that advice; that advice could apply to all leaders for their organization's enhancements.

References

Shafritz, Jay, M. (2009). *Introducing Public Administration, 6ᵗʰ Edition*, Pearson Learning Solutions

Crosby, Barbara C.(2005). *Leadership for the Common Good: Tackling Public Problems in a Shared-Power World, 2ⁿᵈ Edition*, Jossey-Bass

http://www.princeton.edu/~achaney/tmve/wiki100k/docs/Personality_psychology.html

Halley, Henry H. (1965). Halley's Bible Handbook, Zondervan

The Holy Bible, King James Version

Bruce, F.F. et al. (1979). Bible Commentary, Zondervan

Crosby, Barbara C. (2005). *Leadership for the Common Good: Tackling Public Problems in a Shared-Power World, 2ⁿᵈ Edition*, Jossey-Bass

http://www.rose-hulman.edu/studentAffairs/ra/files/CLSK/PDF

www.britannica.com

Ramsbotham, Oliver, WoodHouse, Tom, & Miall, Hugh (2010). Contemporary Conflict Resolution, Second Edition, Polity

Barnett, Michael (2002). Eyewitness To A Genocide, Cornell University Press

http://www.regent.edu/acad/global/publications/ijls/new/vol2iss3/choi/Choi_Vol2Iss3.pdf

Griswold, Wendy (2012). *Cultures and Societies in a Changing World, 4th Edition*, SAGE Publications, Inc

http://www.britannica.com/EBchecked/topic/361645/Nelson-Mandela/282997/Presidency-and-retirement

http://www.rose-hulman.edu/StudentAffairs/ra/files/CLSK/PDF/

https://www.dhs.gov/creation-department-homeland-security

www.wikipedia.org/wiki/list-of-attacks-against-African-American-churches

04090078-00836402

Printed in the United States
By Bookmasters